KIDS ONLY snacks

Company's Coming
COOKBOOKS

Kids Only - Snacks

First printing August 1997
Canadian Cataloguing in Publication Data
Main entry under title:
    Snacks
Issued also in French under title: Les collations.
Includes index.
For children aged 8-15.
ISBN 1-896891-14-4
    1. Snack foods—Juvenile literature. 2. Cookery—
Juvenile literature

TX740.S62 1997   j641.5'3   C97-900368-7

Published simultaneously in Canada and the
United States of America by
The Recipe Factory Inc.
in conjunction with
Company's Coming Publishing Limited
2311 - 96 Street
Edmonton, Alberta, Canada T6N 1G3
Tel: 403 • 450-6223 Fax: 403 • 450-1857

Company's Coming is a registered trademark owned by
Company's Coming Publishing Limited

Front Cover Photo:
Cracker Nachos, page 19
Salsa Pizza, page 68

Back Cover Photo:
1. Cheese 'N' Seed Pinwheels, page 47
2. Fruit Roll Tortillas, page 82
3. Tomato Mozza Rounds, page 69
4. Cheese Crisps, page 17
5. Marshmallow Nests, page 62

Kids Only - Snacks

*was created thanks to the dedicated efforts of the
people and organizations listed below.*

COMPANY'S COMING PUBLISHING LIMITED

Chairperson	Jean Paré
President	Grant Lovig
Production Manager	Kathy Knowles
Production Coordinator	Derrick Sorochan
Design	Nora Cserny
Typesetting	Marlene Crosbie
Copywriting/Project Assistant	Debbie Dixon

THE RECIPE FACTORY INC.

Managing Editor	Nora Prokop
Test Kitchen Supervisor	Lynda Elsenheimer
Assistant Editor/Food Stylist	Stephanie With
Photographer	Stephe Tate Photo
Prop Stylist	Gabriele McEleney

Our special thanks to the following businesses for providing
extensive props for photography.

Chintz & Company	Enchanted Kitchen
Scona Clayworks	Le Gnome
Creations by Design	Libicz's kitchen essentials
Dufferin Game Room Store	Off The Wall Gallery
Eaton's	Stokes
Edmonton Wedding & Party Centre	The Bay

Color separations, printing, and binding by
Friesens, Altona, Manitoba, Canada
Printed in Canada

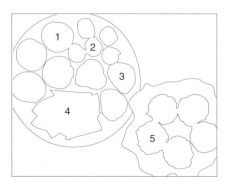

table of contents

foreword

etting hungry? Well, the solution is right here in your hands—an easy-to-follow cookbook filled with recipes for all kinds of great snacks.

This book is set up so that you can let loose in the kitchen without bugging Mom or Dad for help. The handy **Get Ready! Get Set!** list has all the equipment and utensils you'll need, in the order you'll use them. Just follow the easy step-by-step method and—voilà—you have a delicious, hot or cold snack.

You'll see that some recipes have a special icon beside their name —here's what they mean:

chill At some point before serving you'll have to chill this recipe in the refrigerator.

freeze You'll have to freeze this recipe at some point before serving.

hot This recipe has to be baked in the oven. (Don't forget the oven mitts!)

Now that you're ready to get wild in the kitchen, can we make one more suggestion? While it's cool to cook, make sure you clean up when you're done. Your parents will think you're even more terrific than you already are!

watch out! safety in the kitchen tips

1 Never touch anything electrical with wet hands.

2 Always pull out a plug by holding and pulling on the plug itself, not the cord.

3 Keep saucepan handles turned inward on top of the stove.

4 Know how to properly use all appliances before starting.

5 Handle hot plates and dishes with well-insulated oven mitts.

6 Turn off burners and oven, and unplug small appliances when not in use.

4

A note to parents *This book is intended for your children to use. It has been especially written for kids aged 8 to 15 years. Please supervise them when necessary. The handling of sharp knives, boiling liquids, and hot pans needs to be monitored carefully with younger children.*

glossary

Bake   To cook in an oven preheated to the temperature it says in the recipe. Use either the bottom rack or center rack.

Barbecue Fork   A 2-pronged fork with a longer-than-usual handle and a wooden hand grip.

Batter   A mixture of flour, liquid and other ingredients that can be thin (such as pancake batter) or thick (such as muffin batter).

Beat   To mix 2 or more ingredients with a spoon, fork or electric mixer, using a circular motion, until they are smooth.

Blend   To mix 2 or more ingredients together with a spoon, beater, or electric blender until combined.

Boil   To cook a liquid in a saucepan until bubbles rise in a steady pattern and break on the surface. Steam also starts to rise from the surface.

Broil   To cook under the top heating element in the oven. Use either the top rack or the upper rack.

Break An Egg   Tap the side of the egg on the edge of a bowl or cup to crack the shell. Place the tips of both thumbs in the crack and open the shell.

Chill   To refrigerate until cold.

Chop   To cut food carefully into small pieces with a sharp knife on a cutting board; to chop finely is to cut foods as small as you can.

Combine   To put 2 or more ingredients together.

Cream   To beat an ingredient or combination of ingredients until the mixture is soft, smooth, and "creamy."

Cut In   To combine solid fat (such as butter or margarine) with dry ingredients (such as flour) using a fork or pastry blender until the mixture looks like big crumbs the size of green peas.

Dice   To cut food into small ¼ inch (6 mm) cube-shaped pieces.

Dip (into)   To lower into a liquid either part way or all the way.

glossary

Drain To strain away an unwanted liquid (such as water, fruit juice, or grease) using a colander or strainer. Do this over the kitchen sink or in a bowl. Drain grease into a metal can, refrigerate, then throw away in the garbage after it hardens.

Drizzle To dribble drops or lines of glaze or icing over food in a random manner from tines of a fork or the end of a spoon.

Fold To mix gently using a rubber spatula by cutting down in the center and lifting towards the edge of the bowl. Use a "down, up, over" movement, turning the bowl as you repeat.

Fondue To dip, using a long-handled fondue fork, bite-sized pieces of food (bread, vegetables, meat, or fruit) into a hot mixture (cheese, broth, oil, or chocolate), in a special fondue pot placed at the table.

Garnish To decorate food with edible condiments such as parsley sprigs, fruit slices or vegetable cut-outs.

Heat To make something warm or hot by placing the pan on the stove burner that is turned on to the level it says in the recipe.

Knead To work dough into a smooth putty-like mass by pressing and folding using the heels of your hands.

Let Stand To let a baked product cool down slightly on a wire rack or hot pad, while still in its baking pan.

Mash To squash cooked or very ripe foods with a fork or potato masher.

Melt To heat a solid food such as butter, margarine, cheese or chocolate, until it turns into a liquid. Be careful not to burn it.

Mix (see **Combine**)

Mixing Just Until Moistened To put dry ingredients with liquid ingredients until dry ingredients are just wet. Mixture will still be lumpy.

Process To mix up or cut up in a blender (or food processor) until it is the way it says in the recipe.

Sauté To cook food quickly in a small amount of oil in a skillet, wok, or special sauté pan over direct heat.

Scramble-Fry To brown ground meat in hot oil or other fat using a spoon, fork or pancake lifter to break up the meat into small crumb-like pieces as it cooks.

Scrape To use a rubber spatula to remove as much of a mixture as possible from inside a bowl or saucepan.

Separate An Egg (see **Break An Egg**). Once the shell is open, carefully keep the egg yolk in one half shell and let the egg white drip into a small bowl or cup. Carefully pour the yolk into the other half shell, again letting any egg white drip into the bowl or cup. Be careful that the yolk does not break. Continue until there is no more egg white, except in the bowl or cup.

Simmer To cook liquids in a saucepan over a very low heat on the stove burner so that slow bubbles appear on the surface around the sides of the liquid.

Slice To cut foods such as apples, carrots, tomatoes, meat or bread into thin sections or pieces, using a sharp knife.

Spoon (into) To move ingredients from one container to another, using a spoon to scoop from one and drop into the other.

Spread To cover the surface of one product (generally a more solid food) with another product (generally a softer food such as icing or butter).

Stir To mix 2 or more ingredients with a spoon, using a circular motion.

Toast To brown lightly in a toaster or frying pan or under the broiler in the oven.

Toss To mix salad ingredients lightly with a lifting motion, using two forks, two spoons or salad tongs.

equipment & utensils

Barbecue fork

Baking sheet

Broiler pan

Casserole dish

Colander

Cookie cutters

Cookie sheet

Cutting board

Dry measures

Blender

Electric frying pan

Electric mixer

Frying pan

Grater

Hot pad

Ice-cream scoop

Liquid measures

Measuring spoons

Mixing spoons (long-handled)

Microwave oven

2:23
START

Mixing bowls

Muffin pan

Oblong pan
9 x 13 inches
(22 x 33 cm)

Oven mitts

Pancake lifter

Paper muffin cup

Pastry brush

Pastry blender

Pie plate

Pizza pan

Popsicle mold

Rolling pin

Round pan

Rubber spatula

Saucepan

Sharp knife

Square pan
8" x 8" (20 x 20 cm) or
9" x 9" (22 x 22 cm)

Sieve or strainer

Whisk

Table knife, fork & spoon

Wire rack

Burners

Top Rack

Center Rack

Upper Rack

Bottom Rack

Oven with rack positions

- blender
- liquid measures
- measuring spoons
- dry measures
- ice cream scoop

Cranberry Frosty

This is a wonderfully refreshing drink. So quick and easy, too.

1.	**Cranberry juice cocktail**	**2 cups**	**500 mL**
	Skim milk powder	**2 tbsp.**	**30 mL**
	Ice cubes	**4**	**4**
2.	**Vanilla ice cream**	**1 cup**	**250 mL**

1. Combine the first 3 ingredients in the blender. Process for 30 to 60 seconds, turning blender on and off several times to break up ice cubes.

2. Add the ice cream. Process for 20 to 30 seconds. Serve immediately. Makes 4 cups (1 L).

Pictured on page 11.

- blender
- dry measures
- liquid measures

Banana Berry Yogurt Shake

This makes a nice breakfast drink.

1.	**Plain yogurt**	**1 cup**	**250 mL**
	Honey, liquid or creamed	**¼ cup**	**60 mL**
	Banana	**1**	**1**
	Prepared orange juice	**½ cup**	**125 mL**
2.	**Large frozen strawberries**	**6**	**6**

1. Put the first 4 ingredients into the blender. Process for 30 seconds or until the bananas are smooth.

2. While the blender is processing, add the strawberries, 1 at a time, through the opening in the lid. Process until smooth. Serve immediately. Makes 2½ cups (625 mL).

Pictured on page 11.

From left to right: Orange Julius, page 11; Banana Berry Yogurt Shake, page 10; Peach Melba Float, page 12; Cranberry Frosty, page 10; and Creamy Fruit Slush, page 12.

Orange Julius

Orange and frothy—just like it should be.

1.	Cold water	2½ cups	625 mL
	Large egg (see Note)	1	1
	Skim milk powder	½ cup	125 mL
	Frozen concentrated orange juice	½ x 12 oz.	½ x 341 mL
	Vanilla flavoring	½ tsp.	2 mL
	Granulated sugar (optional)	1 tbsp.	15 mL
2.	Ice cubes	6	6

Get ready, get set!

- blender
- liquid measures
- dry measures
- measuring spoons

1. Combine the first 6 ingredients in the blender. Process for 30 seconds.

2. Add the ice cubes, 1 at a time, through the opening in the lid. Process until smooth and frothy. Serve immediately. Makes 5½ cups (1.3 L).

Note: Keep the egg in the refrigerator until you are ready to use it.

Pictured below.

Peach Melba Float

These flavors explode in your mouth.

- blender
- 3 - 8 oz. glasses
- liquid measures
- long-handled mixing spoon
- ice cream scoop

1.	Canned peach slices, with juice	14 oz.	398 mL
2.	Ginger ale	2¼ cups	560 mL
3.	Raspberry sherbet scoops	3	3

1. Put the peach slices into the blender. Process on high for 15 seconds or until smooth. Divide among the 3 glasses.

2. Pour ¾ cup (175 mL) ginger ale into each glass. Stir to mix.

3. Add 1 scoop of raspberry sherbet to each glass. Serve immediately. Makes 3 floats.

Pictured on page 11.

Creamy Fruit Slush freeze

Eat with a spoon—this is too thick for a straw!

- blender
- ice cube tray
- plastic wrap
- liquid measures
- dry measures

1.	Canned pears, peaches or pineapple, with juice	14 oz.	398 mL
2.	Skim evaporated milk	¾ cup	175 mL
	Granulated sugar (optional)	2 tsp.	10 mL

1. Put the fruit into the blender. Process until smooth. Pour the blended fruit into the ice cube tray. Cover with plastic wrap. Freeze.

2. Put the milk and the sugar into the blender. Process until frothy. Add the fruit cubes, 1 at a time, through the opening in the lid. Process until smooth. Serve immediately. Makes 3 cups (750 mL).

Pictured on page 11.

Peanut Butter 'N' Banana Shake

A must for peanut butter lovers.

1.			
Milk	1 cup	250 mL
Skim milk powder	2 tbsp.	30 mL
Large egg (see Note)	1	1
Banana	1	1
Smooth peanut butter	2 tbsp.	30 mL
Ice cubes	3	3
Granulated sugar (optional)	1 tbsp.	15 mL

- blender
- liquid measures
- measuring spoons

1. Put all 7 ingredients into the blender. Process on high for 30 seconds. Let stand 2 seconds. Process again until the ice cubes are crushed. Serve immediately. Makes 2 cups (500 mL).

Note: Keep the egg in the refrigerator until you are ready to use it.

Cinnamon Cider

So comforting after a long day at school. The candies give the drink a pretty rosy glow.

- microwave-safe mug
- liquid measures
- measuring spoons
- mixing spoon
- microwave oven

1.	Apple juice	1 cup	250 mL
	Cinnamon heart candies	1 tbsp.	15 mL
	Cinnamon stick or thin candy stick, for stirring	1	1

1. Pour the apple juice into the mug. Add the cinnamon candies. Stir. Microwave on medium (50%) for about 4 minutes. (Be sure to watch the drink so that it does not boil over. The time will vary with different microwave ovens). Stir with the cinnamon stick. Makes 1 cup (250 mL).

Pictured on page 15.

Spicy Cider

Great for a quick warm-up after skating. What an easy way to get a mulled-cider taste!

- small saucepan
- liquid measures
- measuring spoons
- mixing spoon
- 2 mugs

1.	Apple juice	2 cups	500 mL
	Flavored iced tea crystals	1 tbsp.	15 mL
2.	Ground nutmeg, sprinkle		
	Ground cinnamon, sprinkle		
	Cinnamon sticks or thin candy sticks, for stirring	2	2

1. Heat the apple juice and the iced tea crystals in the saucepan over medium heat.

2. Add the nutmeg and cinnamon. Stir. Heat until steaming. Pour into the 2 mugs. Put 1 cinnamon stick into each mug to stir. Makes 2 cups (500 mL).

Pictured on page 15.

Beverages from left to right: Cinnamon Cider, page 14;
Hot Chocolate For One, page 16; and Spicy Cider, page 14.
Cookies from left to right: Snowballs, page 23; Krispie Oatmeal
Cookies, page 26; and Butterscotch Pudding Cookies, page 27.

Hot Chocolate For One

Great for a cold winter warm-up after school!

- large 12 oz. (375 mL) microwave-safe mug
- measuring spoons
- liquid measures
- microwave oven
- mixing spoon

1.	Cocoa powder (not instant chocolate drink mix)	1 tbsp.	15 mL
	Granulated sugar	1 tbsp.	15 mL
2.	Water	¾ cup	175 mL
3.	Skim evaporated milk	⅔ cup	150 mL
4.	Vanilla flavoring	¾ tsp.	4 mL
	Miniature marshmallows, for garnish		

1. Combine the cocoa powder and sugar in the mug.

2. Put the water in the 1 cup (250 mL) liquid measure. Microwave on high (100%) for 1½ minutes or until it boils. Pour the hot water slowly into the cocoa mixture. Stir until smooth.

3. Pour the milk into the same liquid measure. Microwave on high (100%) for 1 minute. Pour the warm milk into the mug.

4. Add the vanilla. Stir well. Place the marshmallows on top. Serves 1.

Pictured on page 15.

Cucumber Snacks

Couldn't be quicker or easier!

1.			
Process cheese slice	1	1
Soda crackers or stoned wheat thin crackers	4	4
English cucumber slices, with peel	4	4

1. Cut the cheese slice into 4 squares. Place 1 cheese square on top of each cracker. Top each cheese square with a cucumber slice. Makes 4 snacks.

Get ready, get set!

- sharp knife

Cheese Crisps

You could munch on these all day.

1.			
Olive oil	1 tbsp.	15 mL
Garlic powder	¼ tsp.	1 mL
Dried sweet basil	¼ tsp.	1 mL
2. White or whole wheat flour tortillas (8 inch, 20 cm)	3	3
3. Grated Parmesan cheese	3 tbsp.	50 mL

1. Turn the oven on to 375°F (190°C). Combine the first 3 ingredients in the cup.

2. Lay the tortillas out flat on the cutting board. Brush the oil mixture on the tortillas with the brush.

3. Sprinkle with the Parmesan cheese. Cut each tortilla into 8 wedges. Put the wedges on the ungreased baking sheet. Bake on the center rack in the oven for 8 to 10 minutes or until crisp. Use the oven mitts to remove the baking sheet to the wire rack. Eat as is or dip in salsa or Hot Bean Dip, page 34. Makes 24 wedges.

Pictured on the back cover.

Get ready, get set!

- measuring spoons
- small cup
- cutting board
- pastry brush
- pizza cutter or sharp knife
- baking sheet
- oven mitts
- wire rack

Celery Snack chill

These are pretty when they are sliced.

- paper towel
- measuring spoons
- table knife
- plastic wrap
- cutting board
- sharp knife

1.	Celery stalks, 4-6 inches (10-15 cm) long	2	2
2.	Spreadable cream cheese (plain, herb and garlic or pineapple) or process cheese spread (such as CheezWhiz)	1 tbsp.	15 mL

1. Dry the celery stalks well with the paper towel.

2. Fill the hollows of the celery with the cream cheese. Place the celery pieces together to make a tube of cream cheese in the middle. Wrap in plastic wrap. Refrigerate for 1 hour. Cut into bite-size pieces on the cutting board. Makes 1 stuffed celery.

Pictured on page 20.

Cheez 'N' Bacon Snacks hot

Enjoy these warm from the oven.

- measuring spoons
- table knife
- baking sheet
- oven mitts
- wire rack

1.	Process cheese spread (such as CheezWhiz)	2 tbsp.	30 mL
	White bread slices	2	2
2.	Ketchup, approximately	2 tsp.	10 mL
	Simulated bacon bits (or crisp cooked bacon, crumbled)	2 tbsp.	30 mL

1. Put the oven rack in the top position. Turn the oven on to 500°F (260°C). Spread 1 tbsp. (15 mL) of cheese spread on each slice of bread. Cut each slice into 4 squares.

2. Squeeze a dot of ketchup on each piece. Sprinkle with the bacon bits. Place the pieces on the ungreased baking sheet. Broil for about 1½ minutes, or until the cheese is melted and bubbling. Watch carefully. Use the oven mitts to remove the baking sheet to the wire rack. Makes 8 pieces.

Pictured on page 20.

Cheese Snacks

Cracker Nachos (hot)

A very easy whole wheat version of nachos.

1.	Triscuit crackers	20	20
2.	Grated Cheddar cheese	½ cup	125 mL
	Green onions, sliced	2	2
	Green pepper, finely chopped	½	½
	Simulated bacon bits (or crisp cooked bacon, crumbled)	2 tbsp.	30 mL
	Grated Cheddar cheese	½ cup	125 mL
3.	Salsa (mild, medium or hot), optional		

1. Turn the oven on to 350°F (175°C). Place the crackers close together in the ungreased pan.

2. Sprinkle the first amount of cheese, onion, green pepper and bacon bits over top of the crackers. Sprinkle with the second amount of cheese. Bake, uncovered, on the center rack in the oven for 15 minutes. Use the oven mitts to remove the pan to the wire rack.

3. Top with the salsa. Serves 2-4.

Pictured below and on the front cover.

- 9 x 9 inch (22 × 22 cm) pan
- dry measures
- measuring spoons
- oven mitts
- wire rack

Cheese Snacks

19

Cheese Chips hot

Eat these instead of potato chips.

1.	Pita breads (7 inch, 17.5 cm size)	2	2
	No-stick cooking spray		
	Dry grated Cheddar cheese powder	2 tbsp.	30 mL

- baking sheet
- sharp knife
- cutting board
- measuring spoons
- fine sieve
- oven mitts
- wire rack

1. Turn the oven on to 300°F (150°C). Grease the baking sheet. Cut the pitas into 8 wedges each on the cutting board. Split each wedge apart. Place all the pita wedges on the baking sheet. Spray the pita wedges lightly with the no-stick cooking spray. Sprinkle 1 tbsp. (15 mL) of the cheese with the sieve over the pita wedges. Bake on the center rack in the oven for 5 minutes. Use the oven mitts to remove the baking sheet to the wire rack. Carefully turn over each wedge. Spray this side with the no-stick cooking spray. Sprinkle the remaining 1 tbsp. (15 mL) cheese over the pita wedges. Return to the oven and bake for 5 minutes more or until crisp but not brown. Use the oven mitts to remove the baking sheet to the wire rack. Makes 32 pita chips.

Pictured below.

Cheese Snacks

Garlic Cheese Toasts hot

These are crisp and delicious. Great served with soup.

1.	**Soft tub margarine**	**2 tbsp.**	**30 mL**
	Garlic powder	**½ tsp.**	**2 mL**
	Dry grated Cheddar cheese powder	**1 tbsp.**	**15 mL**
2.	**White or whole wheat bread slices**	**4**	**4**

1. Turn the oven on to 350°F (175°C). Combine the margarine, garlic powder and cheese in the bowl. Mix well.

2. Spread the cheese mixture on the slices of bread. Cut each slice into 3 long pieces. Place on the ungreased baking sheet. Bake on the center rack in the oven for 15 minutes or until lightly toasted. Use the oven mitts to remove the baking sheet to the wire rack to cool. Makes 12 snacks.

- measuring spoons
- small bowl
- mixing spoon
- table knife
- baking sheet
- oven mitts
- wire rack

From left to right:
Cheese Devils, page 22
Cheese 'N' Bacon Snacks, page 18
Cheese Chips, page 20
Celery Snack, page 18

Cheese Devils (hot)

A toasted cheese sandwich with some "mystery guests".

1.	**Grated Cheddar cheese**	½ cup	125 mL
	Large egg, fork beaten	1	1
	Salt	½ tsp.	2 mL
	Worcestershire sauce	½ tsp.	2 mL
	Dry mustard powder	1 tsp.	5 mL
2.	**White or whole wheat bread slices (toasted or fresh)**	6	6
3.	**Paprika, sprinkle**		

- small bowl
- dry measures
- measuring spoons
- mixing spoon
- table knife
- baking sheet
- oven mitts
- wire rack

1. Turn the oven on to 400°F (205°C). Measure the first 5 ingredients into the bowl. Mix together well.

2. Spread 1 rounded tablespoon of cheese mixture on each bread slice.

3. Sprinkle lightly with the paprika. Place on the ungreased baking sheet. Bake on the center rack in the oven for 8 minutes or until the cheese is melted. Use the oven mitts to remove the baking sheet to the wire rack. Makes 6 snacks.

Pictured on page 20.

Classic Cheese And Crackers

Make in the microwave. Easy as A,B,C.

1.	**Soda crackers or stoned wheat thins**	6	6
	Thinly sliced Cheddar cheese, to fit crackers		
	Whole oregano, sprinkle (optional)		

- medium microwave-safe plate
- microwave oven

1. Arrange the cheese slices on the crackers. Sprinkle with the oregano. Place on the plate. Microwave on high (100 %) for 40 to 45 seconds or until the cheese is melted. Makes 6 crackers.

Snowballs

Crunchy and sweet (and full of fiber).

1.	**Butter or hard margarine**	**½ cup**	**125 mL**
	Chopped pitted dates	**2 cups**	**500 mL**
	Water	**¼ cup**	**60 mL**
	Ground cinnamon	**⅛ tsp.**	**0.5 mL**
2.	**Chopped walnuts or pecans (optional)**	**½ cup**	**125 mL**
	Granola cereal	**½ cup**	**125 mL**
	Crisp rice cereal	**½ cup**	**125 mL**
3.	**Angel flake (fancy flake) coconut, see Note**	**¾ cup**	**175 mL**

Get ready, get set!

- medium saucepan
- dry measures
- liquid measures
- measuring spoons
- mixing spoon
- hot pad
- small bowl
- waxed paper

1. Melt the butter in the saucepan over medium heat. Add the dates, water and cinnamon. Stir. Cook over medium heat until the mixture is bubbling. Reduce the heat to low. Stir for 5 minutes or until the mixture is thick. Remove the saucepan to the hot pad. Cool for 10 minutes.

2. Add the nuts, granola and rice cereal. Mix well.

3. Put the coconut into the small bowl. Wet your hands with water. Roll mixture into 1 inch (2.5 cm) balls with your hands. Roll the balls in the coconut. Place on the waxed paper on the counter. Serve at room temperature or chilled. Store in a covered container in the refrigerator. Makes 30 balls.

Note: You can substitute medium thread coconut for the angel flake.

Pictured on page 15.

Triple Chocolate Chip Cookies hot

Only for chocolate lovers.

Get ready, get set!

- cookie sheet
- large bowl
- dry measures
- mixing spoon
- small table spoon
- oven mitts
- wire rack
- pancake lifter or metal spatula
- waxed paper

1.			
Chocolate cake mix, 2 layer size	1	1
Sour cream	1 cup	250 mL
Large eggs	2	2
Box of instant chocolate pudding powder (4 serving size)	1	1
Chocolate chips (mini, regular or jumbo)	1 cup	250 mL

1. Turn the oven on to 350°F (175°C). Grease the cookie sheet. Combine all 5 ingredients in the bowl. Stir until moistened and no big lumps remain. Drop by rounded spoonfuls, about 2 inches (5 cm) apart, onto the cookie sheet. Bake on the center rack in the oven for 16 to 18 minutes. Use the oven mitts to remove the cookie sheet to the wire rack. Let stand for 2 minutes. Use the pancake lifter to remove the cookies to the waxed paper on the counter. Cool completely. Makes about 4 dozen.

RAINBOW CHOCOLATE COOKIES: Use multi-colored baking chips instead of the chocolate chips.

Corn Flakes Macaroons (hot)

Careful or the adults will eat all of these.

1.	Egg whites (large), see Note	3	3
2.	Granulated sugar	⅔ cup	150 mL
	Vanilla flavoring	1 tsp.	5 mL
	Corn flakes cereal	2 cups	500 mL
	Angel flake (fancy flake) or long thread coconut	1 cup	250 mL

1. Turn the oven on to 325°F (160°C). Beat the egg whites on high speed in the bowl until foamy and fluffy.

2. Gradually add the sugar. Add the vanilla. Beat until shiny and stiff peaks form. (When you lift the beaters, the peaks should not fold over). Fold in the corn flakes and the coconut using the spatula. Cover the ungreased cookie sheet with the waxed paper. Drop by spoonfuls onto the baking sheet. Bake on the center rack in the oven for 20 minutes or until lightly browned and crisp. Use the oven mitts to remove the cookie sheet to the wire rack. Let stand for 2 minutes. Use the pancake lifter to remove the cookies to the wire rack. Cool completely. Makes 30 cookies.

Note: See Separating Eggs in the Glossary, page 7. As a suggestion, the egg yolks can be used in Banana Pudding, page 95.

Pictured below.

Get ready, get set!

- large bowl
- electric mixer
- dry measures
- measuring spoons
- rubber spatula
- cookie sheet
- waxed paper
- small table spoon
- oven mitts
- wire rack
- pancake lifter or metal spatula

Krispie Oatmeal Cookies

These chewy cookies are loaded with raisins or chips.

- cookie sheet
- medium bowl
- dry measures
- mixing spoon
- measuring spoons
- small table spoon
- oven mitts
- wire rack
- pancake lifter or metal spatula
- waxed paper

1.	Butter or hard margarine, softened	¹/₂ cup	125 mL
	Brown sugar, packed	¹/₂ cup	125 mL
	Granulated sugar	¹/₂ cup	125 mL
2.	Large egg	1	1
	Vanilla flavoring	1 tsp.	5 mL
3.	All-purpose flour	1 cup	250 mL
	Baking soda	¹/₂ tsp.	2 mL
4.	Rolled oats (not instant)	1 cup	250 mL
	Crisp rice cereal	1 cup	250 mL
	Raisins, chocolate chips or multi-colored baking chips	1 cup	250 mL

1. Turn the oven on to 350°F (175°C). Grease the cookie sheet. Cream the butter and the sugars in the bowl.

2. Add the egg and the vanilla. Stir.

3. Add the flour and the baking soda. Mix with the spoon until blended.

4. Stir in the rolled oats, rice cereal and raisins. Drop by rounded spoonfuls, about 2 inches (5 cm) apart, onto the cookie sheet. Bake on the center rack in the oven for 12 minutes or until golden. Use the oven mitts to remove the cookie sheet to the wire rack. Let stand for 2 minutes. Use the pancake lifter to remove the cookies to the waxed paper on the counter. Cool completely. Makes 45 cookies.

Pictured on page 15.

Butterscotch Pudding Cookies

A very fast and easy way to make cookies.

1.			
Butter or hard margarine, melted	2 tbsp.	30 mL	
Large egg, fork-beaten	1	1	
Box of instant butterscotch pudding powder (4 serving size)	1	1	
Biscuit mix	1 cup	250 mL	
Milk	1 tbsp.	15 mL	

1. Turn the oven on to 350°F (175°C). Combine all 5 ingredients in the bowl. Mix well. Make balls using 1 tbsp. (15 mL) of dough. Place 3 inches (7.5 cm) apart on the ungreased cookie sheet. Make a criss-cross pattern with the fork. Bake on the center rack in the oven for 8 minutes. Use the oven mitts to remove the cookie sheet to the wire rack. Let stand for 2 minutes. Use the pancake lifter to remove the cookies to the waxed paper on the counter. Cool completely. Makes 16 cookies.

Variation: Add ½ cup (125 mL) chopped pecans or walnuts for a nutty taste.

Pictured on page 15.

Get ready, get set!

- medium bowl
- measuring spoons
- dry measures
- mixing spoon
- cookie sheet
- table fork
- oven mitts
- wire rack
- pancake lifter or metal spatula
- waxed paper

Caesar Dip

If you like caesar salad, you will love this. Dip any vegetable. Especially good with the crisp center leaves of romaine lettuce.

- small bowl
- dry measures
- measuring spoons
- whisk

1.			
Mayonnaise (or salad dressing)	½ cup	125 mL
Sour cream	½ cup	125 mL
Lemon juice, fresh or bottled	1 tbsp.	15 mL
Garlic clove, crushed (or use ¼ tsp., 1 mL powder)	1	1
Salt	⅛ tsp.	0.5 mL
Pepper	⅛ tsp.	0.5 mL
Prepared mustard	1 tsp.	5 mL
Grated Parmesan cheese	1 tbsp.	15 mL
Parsley flakes	1 tsp.	5 mL

1. Whisk all 9 ingredients together in the bowl. Let the dip stand for 15 minutes to blend flavors. Makes ¾ cup (175 mL).

Toast Spread

Spread on hot toast, bagels or biscuits. Try as an ice cream topping, too!

- small bowl
- dry measures
- mixing spoon

1.			
Jar marshmallow cream topping (6 oz., 200 g size)	1	1
Fruit Spread (available in the jam section at the grocery store)	1 cup	250 mL

1. Combine the marshmallow cream with the fruit spread in the bowl. Mix well. Ready to use. Store any remaining spread in a covered container in the refrigerator for up to 2 weeks. Makes 2 cups (500 mL).

Cream Cheese Spread

Very smooth and creamy.

1.	Cream cheese, softened	8 oz.	250 g
2.	Your favorite flavored gelatin (jelly powder), 4 serving size	3 oz.	85 g
	Milk	1/4 cup	60 mL

1. Beat the cream cheese on medium speed in the bowl until smooth.

2. Add the gelatin and milk. Beat until smooth. Spread on bagels, crackers or toast. Store any remaining spread in a covered container in the refrigerator for up to 2 weeks. Makes 1³/₄ cups (425 mL).

Variation: To make a fruit or cake dip, fold the cream cheese and gelatin into 16 oz. (500 g) of non-dairy frozen whipped topping (such as Cool Whip), thawed.

- medium bowl
- electric mixer
- liquid measures

Creamy Yogurt Dip

Use with fresh vegetables or Crispy Potato Wedges, page 74.

1.	Thick plain yogurt	1/4 cup	60 mL
	Mayonnaise (or salad dressing)	1/4 cup	60 mL
	Granulated sugar	1 tsp.	5 mL
	Salt, sprinkle		
	Pepper, sprinkle		

- small bowl
- dry measures
- measuring spoons
- mixing spoon

1. Combine all 5 ingredients in the bowl. Mix well. Makes 1/2 cup (125 mL).

Honey Mustard Dip

Use for veggies, fish sticks and chicken fingers.

- small bowl
- dry measures
- measuring spoons
- mixing spoon

1.			
Sour cream		½ cup	125 mL
Liquid honey		1 tbsp.	15 mL
Prepared mustard		2 tsp.	10 mL

1. Combine all 3 ingredients in the bowl. Mix well. Makes ½ cup (125 mL).

Pictured below.

Counter clockwise from top right: Taffy Fruit Dip, page 31;
Honey Mustard Dip, page 30; and Honey Lime Fruit Dip, page 31.

Dips & Spreads

Taffy Fruit Dip

Especially delicious with apple wedges. Like taffy apples.

1.			
Cream cheese, softened	4 oz.	125 g
Brown sugar, packed	½ cup	125 mL
Vanilla flavoring	2 tsp.	10 mL

2.			
Chopped peanuts (optional)	¼ cup	60 mL
Fresh fruit, for dipping		

- medium bowl
- dry measures
- measuring spoons
- electric mixer

1. Beat the first 3 ingredients together in the bowl on medium speed until smooth and fluffy and the sugar is dissolved.

2. Stir in the peanuts. Dip fresh fruit into the taffy dip. Store any remaining dip in the refrigerator. It will stiffen slightly. Soften in microwave oven on low (20%) power for just a few seconds. Makes ¾ cup (175 mL).

Pictured on page 30.

Honey Lime Fruit Dip chill

Very refreshing. Great for dipping berries, grapes, melon, banana and apples.

1.			
Sour cream (or thick plain yogurt)	1 cup	250 mL
Liquid honey	2 tbsp.	30 mL
Grated peel and juice of 1 lime		
Poppy seeds (optional)	½ tsp.	2 mL

- small bowl
- dry measures
- measuring spoons
- mixing spoon

1. Combine all 4 ingredients in the bowl. Mix. Chill in the refrigerator for about 5 minutes to blend the flavors. Makes 1 cup (250 mL).

Pictured on page 30.

Tomato Cheese Fondue

Invite two friends over for a fondue after school and get your homework done while indulging.

- medium microwave-safe bowl
- dry measures
- measuring spoons
- mixing spoon
- waxed paper
- microwave oven

1.			
Tomato sauce	7½ oz.	213 mL
Grated Cheddar cheese	2 cups	500 mL
Onion powder	½ tsp.	2 mL
Garlic salt	¼ tsp.	1 mL
Pepper	¼ tsp.	1 mL

2. Baguette bread slices, halved or quartered or fresh bread sticks

1. Combine the first 5 ingredients in the bowl. Stir. Cover with the waxed paper. Microwave on high (100%) for 1 minute. Stir. Re-cover and microwave on high (100%) for 2 minutes. Stir well.

2. Dip bread into cheese mixture. Makes 1⅓ cups (325 mL).

Dips & Spreads

Hot Mushroom Cheddar Dip

Great to dip nacho chips, veggies or bread. Just like a fondue.

1.	Condensed cream of mushroom soup	10 oz.	284 mL
	Skim evaporated milk	¾ cup	175 mL
	Grated Cheddar cheese	2 cups	500 mL
	Worcestershire sauce	1 tsp.	5 mL
2.	Green onion, sliced	1	1

- medium microwave-safe bowl
- liquid measures
- dry measures
- measuring spoons
- mixing spoon
- microwave oven

1. Combine the first 4 ingredients in the bowl. Stir. Microwave on high (100%) for 2 to 3 minutes. Stir well. Microwave for 30 seconds more or until the cheese is melted.

2. Sprinkle with the green onion. Makes 2 cups (500 mL).

Pictured below.

Dips & Spreads

Hot Bean Dip

Try this dip with Cheese Crisps, page 17 or Crispy Potato Wedges, page 74.

- small saucepan
- dry measures
- mixing spoon
- measuring spoons

1.			
Canned refried beans with chilies (see Note)	½ cup	125 mL
Process cheese spread (such as CheezWhiz) or 2 process cheese slices, cut up	2 tbsp.	30 mL

1. Heat the refried beans in the saucepan over medium heat. Stir in the cheese until melted. Makes ½ cup (125 mL).

Note: If you do not have refried beans with chilies, use plain refried beans plus a sprinkle of cayenne pepper or dried chilies.

Microwave Variation: Put the refried beans into a small microwave-safe bowl. Add the cheese. Cover with waxed paper. Microwave on high (100%) for 30 seconds. Stir and microwave for 30 seconds more until the dip is hot and the cheese is melted.

Dips & Spreads

Frozen Peach Yogurt freeze

Make sure to blend in the yogurt until the mixture is very smooth.

1.	Canned sliced peaches, with juice	2 x 14 oz.	2 x 398 mL
2.	Granulated sugar	3 tbsp.	50 mL
	Envelope unflavored gelatin	2 x ¼ oz.	2 x 7 g
3.	Vanilla-flavored yogurt (or use plain yogurt and add 1 tsp., 5 mL vanilla flavoring)	2 cups	500 mL
4.	Waxed paper or plastic drink cups (4 oz., 125 mL size)	10	10
	Wooden popsicle sticks (available at craft stores)	10	10

- strainer
- medium bowl
- medium saucepan
- measuring spoons
- long-handled mixing spoon
- dry measures
- hot pad
- potato masher

1. Place the strainer over the bowl. Pour the peaches into the strainer. Let stand for 3 minutes or until all the juice has drained into the bowl.

2. Pour the juice into the saucepan. Stir in the sugar and the gelatin. Heat over medium-high heat until just starting to boil. Remove the saucepan to the hot pad and stir the mixture until the sugar and the gelatin are dissolved. Mash the peaches with the potato masher or blend in a blender until the peaches are chunky. Add the peaches to the hot juice.

3. Add the yogurt. Mix well.

4. Fill the cups to the brim and insert the sticks. Freeze. To remove, run hot water on the bottom of the cup until the frozen yogurt slides out. Makes 5 cups (1.25 L) of yogurt mixture, enough for 10 popsicles.

Creamy Hawaiian Freezies freeze

Very tropical.

- blender
- liquid measures
- dry measures
- measuring spoons
- plastic popsicle container

1.	Canned crushed pineapple, with juice	14 oz.	398 mL
	Liquid honey	¼ cup	60 mL
	Banana, cut in chunks	1	1
	Long thread coconut	½ cup	125 mL
	Coconut flavoring	1 tsp.	5 mL
	Skim evaporated milk	⅔ cup	150 mL
	Drop of yellow food coloring (optional)	1	1

1. Combine all 7 ingredients in the blender. Process until smooth. Pour into the popsicle container. Insert the tops. Freeze. To remove, run the container quickly under hot water. Makes 15 popsicles (2 oz., 60 mL each).

Banana Popsicles freeze

Really quick to make. The food coloring just punches the color up a bit.

- blender
- liquid measures
- dry measures
- plastic popsicle container

1.	Prepared orange or pineapple juice	2 cups	500 mL
	Skim milk powder	½ cup	125 mL
2.	Ripe bananas, peeled and cut into chunks	3	3
	Yellow food coloring drops (optional)	5	5

1. Combine the juice and the milk powder in the blender. Process on medium for 1 minute.

2. Add the banana, a few chunks at a time, processing on high for 5 seconds after each addition. Add the food coloring. Process for 30 seconds more or until smooth. Pour into the plastic popsicle container. Insert the tops. Freeze. To remove, run the container quickly under hot water. Makes 16 popsicles (2 oz., 60 mL each).

Frozen Treats

Marshmallow Fruit Pops freeze

Marshmallows make this chewy.

1.	Cream cheese, softened	8 oz.	250 g
	Liquid honey	¼ cup	60 mL
2.	Non-dairy frozen whipped topping (such as Cool Whip)	2 cups	500 mL
	Chopped fresh fruit (or use frozen fruit, thawed with juice or canned fruit, with juice)	2 cups	500 mL
3.	Miniature marshmallows (white or colored)	3 cups	750 mL
	Waxed paper or plastic drink cups (4 oz., 125 mL size)	9	9
	Wooden popsicle sticks (available at craft stores)	9	9

1. Beat the cream cheese and the honey in the bowl on medium speed until smooth.

2. Add the whipped topping and the fruit. Beat on low speed.

3. Add the marshmallows. Stir. Fill the cups ⅔ full. Insert the sticks. Freeze. To remove, peel the paper or dip in hot water. Makes 9 fruit pops.

Get ready, get set!

- small bowl
- liquid measures
- electric mixer
- dry measures
- mixing spoon

- medium saucepan
- liquid measures
- hot pad
- long handled mixing spoon
- dry measures

Apple Lime Freezies freeze

The color is great! And the lime taste is refreshing.

1.	Apple juice	2 cups	500 mL
2.	Lime-flavored gelatin (jelly powder), 4 serving size	3 oz.	85 g
3.	Apple juice	2 cups	500 mL
	Apple sauce	1 cup	250 mL
4.	Waxed paper or plastic drink cups (5 oz., 140 g size)	10	10
	Wooden popsicle sticks (available at craft stores), see Note	10	10

1. Pour the first amount of apple juice into the saucepan. Heat over medium-high heat until just starting to boil.

2. Remove the saucepan to the hot pad. Add the lime gelatin. Stir until dissolved.

3. Add the second amount of apple juice and the apple sauce. Stir.

4. Pour the mixture into the drink cups to ¾ full. Freeze. Add the sticks. To remove, run hot water on the bottom of the cup until the freezie slides out. Makes 10 popsicles.

Note: To have the sticks stay upright, place a piece of foil over each cup and cut a small slit in the middle. Fit the sticks in through the foil.

Pictured below.

Choco Peanut Butter Dreams, page 39. Apple Lime Freezies, page 38.

Frozen Treats

Choco Peanut Butter Dream *freeze*

That wonderful combination of chocolate and peanut butter. A great treat to have in the freezer.

1.	**Envelope dessert topping (such as Dream Whip)**	1	1
	Milk	½ cup	125 mL
2.	**Smooth peanut butter**	½ cup	125 mL
3.	**Milk**	1 cup	250 mL
	Instant chocolate pudding powder, 4 serving size	1	1
4.	**Chocolate wafers (6 oz., 200 g package)**	48	48

- medium bowl
- liquid measures
- electric mixer
- dry measures
- baking sheet
- small table spoon
- sealable freezer bag

1. Combine the whipped topping and the first amount of milk together in the bowl. Beat on high speed until thickened.

2. Add the peanut butter. Beat on low speed until mixed.

3. Add the second amount of milk and the pudding powder. Beat on low speed until blended. Beat on high speed for 2 minutes.

4. Place 24 of the wafers on the ungreased baking sheet. Put a heaping spoonful of the mixture on each wafer. Top with the remaining 24 wafers. Freeze, uncovered, for 3 hours. Put in a covered container to store. Makes 24 "dreams".

Pictured on page 38.

Orange Cranberry Muffins hot

Using the entire orange gives these muffins lots of vitamins and minerals.

Get ready, get set!

- muffin pan (for 12 muffins)
- sharp knife
- blender
- liquid measures
- dry measures
- large bowl
- mixing spoon
- measuring spoons
- wooden toothpick
- oven mitts
- wire rack

1.			
Medium navel orange	1	1
Prepared orange juice	½ cup	125 mL
Large egg	1	1
Butter or hard margarine	½ cup	125 mL
Dried cranberries (see Note)	½ cup	125 mL
2.			
All-purpose flour	1¾ cups	425 mL
Baking powder	1 tsp.	5 mL
Baking soda	1 tsp.	5 mL
Granulated sugar	⅔ cup	150 mL
Salt	½ tsp.	2 mL

1. Turn the oven on to 400°F (205°C). Grease the muffin pan. Cut the orange into 8 pieces. Place in the blender. Add the orange juice. Process for 1½ minutes or until the orange peel is finely chopped. Add the egg and the butter. Process until blended. Add the dried cranberries and process for 2 seconds.

2. Combine the next 5 ingredients in the large bowl. Mix. Make a well in the center. Pour the wet ingredients into the well. Stir to moisten. Do not stir too much. Divide the batter between the 12 muffin cups. Bake on the center rack in the oven for 15 minutes or until golden. The toothpick inserted in the center of 2 or 3 muffins should come out clean. Use the oven mitts to remove the muffin pan to the wire rack. Let stand for 10 minutes then remove the muffins to the rack to cool completely. Makes 12 muffins.

Note: Frozen cranberries can be substituted for the dried, however, the muffins will be green in color.

Pictured on page 45.

Muffins, etc.

Date & Nut Muffins

A great snack for any time of the day.

1.			
	All-purpose flour	1½ cups	375 mL
	Whole wheat flour	½ cup	125 mL
	Baking powder	1 tbsp.	15 mL
	Brown sugar, packed	¼ cup	60 mL
	Chopped walnuts	½ cup	125 mL
2.			
	Milk	1 cup	250 mL
	Large egg	1	1
	Cooking oil	¼ cup	60 mL
	Maple flavoring	½ tsp.	2 mL
	Chopped dates	½ cup	125 mL

- muffin pan (for 12 muffins)
- large bowl
- dry measures
- measuring spoons
- mixing spoon
- blender
- liquid measures
- wooden toothpick
- oven mitts
- wire rack

1. Turn the oven on to 375°F (190°C). Grease the muffin pan. Combine the first 5 ingredients in the bowl. Stir. Make a well in the center.

2. Combine the next 5 ingredients in the blender. Process for 5 to 10 minutes. Pour the wet ingredients into the well. Stir to moisten. Do not stir too much. Divide the batter between the 12 muffin cups. Bake on the center rack in the oven for 20 minutes or until golden. The toothpick inserted in the center of 2 or 3 muffins should come out clean. Use the oven mitts to remove the muffin pan to the wire rack. Let stand for 10 minutes then remove the muffins to the rack to cool completely. Makes 12 muffins.

Pictured below.

P. B. Surprise Muffins

Fun to prepare, fun to eat. These are great served warm.

- muffin pan
  (for 12 muffins)
- medium bowl
- dry measures
- mixing spoon
- liquid measures
- measuring spoons
- large bowl
- wooden toothpick
- oven mitts
- wire rack

1. Crumbled bran flakes cereal	½ cup	125 mL
Butter or hard margarine, melted	¼ cup	60 mL
Peanut butter, smooth or crunchy	½ cup	125 mL
2. Large egg, fork-beaten	1	1
Milk, warmed	1½ cups	375 mL
Vanilla flavoring	1 tsp.	5 mL
3. All-purpose flour	2 cups	500 mL
Baking powder	4 tsp.	20 mL
Salt	1 tsp.	5 mL
Brown sugar, packed	¼ cup	60 mL
4. Jam, your favorite	¼ cup	60 mL

1. Turn the oven on to 400°F (205°C). Grease the muffin pan. Combine the cereal, butter and peanut butter in the bowl. Stir.

2. Add the egg, milk and vanilla. Stir. Let stand for 5 minutes.

3. Combine the next 4 ingredients in the large bowl. Make a well in the center. Pour the wet ingredients into the well. Stir to moisten. Do not stir too much. Divide the batter between the 12 muffin cups.

4. Push 1 tsp. (5 mL) of jam into the top of each muffin. Bake on the center rack in the oven for 20 minutes or until golden. The toothpick inserted in the center of 2 or 3 muffins should come out clean. Use the oven mitts to remove the muffin pan to the wire rack. Let stand for 10 minutes then remove the muffins to the rack to cool completely. Makes 12 muffins.

Muffins, etc.

Lemon Blueberry Muffins

Cake mix makes a very easy start to these muffins.

1.			
Envelope lemon cake mix, 2 layer size		1	1
Large eggs, fork-beaten		2	2
Sour cream		1½ cups	375 mL
Frozen blueberries		2 cups	500 mL

1. Turn the oven on to 325°F (160°C). Place the muffin papers in the pans. Combine the cake mix, eggs and sour cream in the bowl. Stir until well blended. Batter will be stiff. Lightly fold in the blueberries using the spatula. Divide the batter among the 18 muffin cups. Bake on the center rack in the oven for 40 minutes or until golden. The toothpick inserted in the center of 2 or 3 muffins should come out clean. Use the oven mitts to remove the muffin pans. Remove the muffins to the wire rack to cool completely. Makes 18 muffins.

Pictured below.

Get ready, get set!

- 2 muffin pans (for 18 muffins)
- 18 muffin papers
- large bowl
- mixing spoon
- rubber spatula
- dry measures
- wooden toothpick
- oven mitts
- wire rack

Whole Wheat Crazy Bread hot

This will become a favorite in your home.

- 12 inch (30 cm) pizza pan or 10 × 15 inch (25 × 38 cm) baking sheet
- small bowl
- measuring spoons
- dry measures
- mixing spoon
- medium bowl
- liquid measures
- whisk
- clean cloth
- small bowl
- sharp knife
- pastry brush
- oven mitts
- wire rack

1.	Fast-rising instant yeast	1 tbsp.	15 mL
	Whole wheat flour	1 cup	250 mL
2.	Very warm water	1 cup	250 mL
	Cooking oil	1 tbsp.	15 mL
	Granulated sugar	1 tsp.	5 mL
	Salt	1 tsp.	5 mL
3.	All-purpose flour	1½ cups	375 mL
4.	Butter or hard margarine, melted	2 tbsp.	30 mL
	Garlic powder	⅛ tsp.	0.5 mL
	Dried sweet basil	1 tsp.	5 mL
5.	Grated Parmesan cheese	2 tbsp.	30 mL

1. Turn the oven on to 400°F (205°C). Grease the pan. Combine the yeast and whole wheat flour in the small bowl. Set aside.

2. Combine the water, cooking oil, sugar and salt in the medium bowl. Stir until dissolved. Add the whole wheat flour mixture. Whisk until smooth.

3. Add the all-purpose flour. Mix well. Cover the bowl with the cloth. Let stand for 15 minutes.

4. Combine the butter, garlic and basil in the small bowl. Knead the flour mixture 3 or 4 times. Press out evenly into the greased pan. Cut into 14 sticks or fingers with a sharp knife. Brush the butter mixture over the surface of the dough.

5. Sprinkle with the Parmesan cheese. Cover the baking sheet with the cloth. Let stand 15 minutes. Bake, uncovered, on the center rack in the oven for 20 minutes or until lightly golden. Use the oven mitts to remove the pan to the wire rack to cool. Makes 14 crazy bread sticks.

Pictured on page 45.

Clockwise from top right: Orange Cranberry Muffins, page 40; Sesame Honeys, page 48; Whole Wheat Crazy Bread, page 44; and Apple Granola Muffins, page 46.

Muffins, etc.

Apple Granola Muffins hot

Moist and delicious.

- muffin pan
  (for 12 muffins)
- medium bowl
- dry measures
- measuring spoons
- mixing spoon
- pastry blender
- liquid measures
- wooden toothpick
- oven mitts
- wire rack

1.			
	All-purpose flour	2 cups	500 mL
	Baking powder	4 tsp.	20 mL
	Salt	1 tsp.	5 mL
	Brown sugar	3 tbsp.	50 mL
	Ground cinnamon	¹/₂ tsp.	2 mL
2.	Butter or hard margarine	¹/₃ cup	75 mL
	Apple, cored and chopped	1	1
	Milk	1 cup	250 mL
	Vanilla flavoring	1 tsp.	5 mL
	Granola cereal or Crumble	¹/₄ cup	60 mL
	Topping, page 96		

1. Turn the oven on to 400°F (205°C). Grease the muffin pan. Combine the first 5 ingredients in the bowl. Stir well.

2. Add the butter. Cut the butter in with the pastry blender until the flour looks crumbly. Add the apple, milk and vanilla. Stir to moisten. Do not stir too much. Divide the batter between the 12 muffin cups. Sprinkle each with 1 tsp. (5 mL) of granola. Bake on the center rack in the oven for 20 minutes or until golden. The toothpick inserted in the center of 2 or 3 muffins should come out clean. Use the oven mitts to remove the muffin pan to the wire rack. Let stand for 10 minutes then remove the muffins to the rack to cool completely. Makes 12 muffins.

Pictured on page 45.

Cheese 'N' Seed Pinwheels (hot)

These are simply scrumptious!

1.	Biscuit mix	2 cups	500 mL
	Grated Cheddar cheese	1/2 cup	125 mL
	Garlic powder	1/4 tsp.	1 mL
	Cold water	2/3 cup	150 mL
2.	Biscuit mix, for rolling	1/4 cup	60 mL
3.	Soft tub margarine	2 tbsp.	30 mL
	Sesame seeds	3 tbsp.	50 mL
	Shelled roasted sunflower seeds	3 tbsp.	50 mL
4.	Milk, for brushing		

1. Turn the oven on to 425°F (220°C). Combine the first amount of biscuit mix, cheese and garlic powder in the bowl. Mix. Add the cold water. Stir with the fork until a soft dough forms. Let stand 5 minutes.

2. Sprinkle the second amount of biscuit mix on the counter or working surface. Place the dough on the biscuit mix. Sprinkle more biscuit mix on top. Knead the dough with your hands 10 times. Use more biscuit mix if the dough is sticky. Roll the dough into a 12 × 12 inch (30 × 30 cm) square.

3. Spread the margarine over top. Sprinkle with the sesame seeds and the sunflower seeds. Roll up like a jelly roll. Pinch the long end to seal. Set on the cutting board. Cut the roll into 1 inch (2.5 cm) slices. Lay flat on the ungreased baking sheet.

4. Brush the top sides with the milk. Bake on the center rack in the oven for 10 to 15 minutes. Use the oven mitts to remove the baking sheet to the wire rack. Makes 12 biscuits.

Pictured on the back cover.

Get ready, get set!

- medium bowl
- dry measures
- measuring spoons
- mixing spoon
- liquid measures
- table fork
- rolling pin
- table knife
- sharp knife
- baking sheet
- pastry brush
- oven mitts
- wire rack

Sesame Honeys hot

These are very tasty. Crisp and chewy.

- large bowl
- dry measures
- measuring spoons
- mixing spoon
- pastry blender
- small bowl
- liquid measures
- rolling pin
- ruler
- sharp knife
- table fork
- cookie sheet
- pancake lifter or metal spatula
- oven mitts
- wire rack
- waxed paper

1.	**Whole wheat flour**	**1 cup**	**250 mL**
	All-purpose flour	**1 cup**	**250 mL**
	Salt	**1 tsp.**	**5 mL**
	Baking powder	**1 tsp.**	**5 mL**
	Sesame seeds	**¹/₂ cup**	**125 mL**
2.	**Butter or hard margarine**	**¹/₄ cup**	**60 mL**
3.	**Liquid honey**	**¹/₂ cup**	**125 mL**
	Milk	**¹/₃ cup**	**75 mL**
4.	**Flour**	**1-2 tbsp.**	**15-30 mL**

1. Turn the oven on to 350°F (175°C). Combine the first 5 ingredients in the large bowl. Mix well.

2. Cut in the butter with the pastry blender until crumbly.

3. Stir the honey and milk together in the small bowl. Add to the flour mixture. Stir until it forms a stiff dough.

4. Sprinkle the flour onto the counter or working surface. Use your hands to form the dough into a flat rectangle. Roll to flatten to a 12 × 15 inch (30 × 38 cm) rectangle that is ¹/₈ to ¹/₄ inch (3 to 6 mm) thick. Cut into 3 inch (7.5 cm) square crackers with the tip of the sharp knife. Use the pancake lifter to place the crackers on the ungreased cookie sheet. Poke each cracker 3 times with the fork. Bake on the center rack in the oven for 15 minutes or until golden. Use the oven mitts to remove the cookie sheet to the wire rack. Let stand 2 minutes. Use the pancake lifter to remove the crackers to the waxed paper on the counter. Cool completely. Makes about 20 crackers.

Pictured on page 45.

Muffins, etc.

Summertime Snack Mix

A sweet mix. Take some in a baggie for a recess snack.

1.	Honey graham cereal squares	2 cups	500 mL
	O-shaped toasted oat cereal	2 cups	500 mL
	Dried banana chips	1 cup	250 mL
2.	Butter or hard margarine, melted	3 tbsp.	50 mL
	Liquid honey	¼ cup	60 mL
	Ground cinnamon	½ tsp.	2 mL
	Lemon juice, fresh or bottled	2 tsp.	10 mL
3.	Chopped dried pineapple	1 cup	250 mL
	Golden raisins	1 cup	250 mL
	Long thread coconut	1 cup	250 mL
	Popped corn (pop about 2 tbsp., 30 mL kernels)	4 cups	1 L

Get ready, get set!

- large microwave-safe bowl
- dry measures
- mixing spoon
- small bowl
- liquid measures
- measuring spoons
- microwave oven
- oven mitts
- hot pad

1. Combine the first 3 ingredients in the large bowl. Stir.

2. Combine the melted butter, honey, cinnamon and lemon juice in the small bowl. Stir. Pour the honey mixture slowly over the cereal mixture. Stir well to coat. Microwave, uncovered, on high (100%) for 2 minutes. Stir well. Continue to microwave on high (100%) for 2 to 3 minutes, stirring at the end of each minute and watching so it does not burn. It should look toasted when done. Use the oven mitts to remove the bowl to the hot pad.

3. Add the pineapple, raisins, coconut and popcorn. Toss together well. Let cool for about 1 hour. Makes 10 cups (2.5 L).

Pictured below.

Peanut Butter & Jelly Popcorn

Much more fun than a peanut butter and jelly sandwich.

- large bowl
- dry measures
- small saucepan
- measuring spoons
- long-handled mixing spoon

1.	Popped corn (pop about ¼ cup, 60 mL kernels)	6 cups	1.5 L
2.	Butter or hard margarine	1 tbsp.	15 mL
	Smooth peanut butter	2 tbsp.	30 mL
	Grape jelly (or your favorite flavor)	2 tbsp.	30 mL

1. Put the popped corn into the bowl.

2. Combine the butter, peanut butter and jelly in the saucepan over medium heat. Stir until melted. Pour the peanut butter mixture over the popcorn. Mix well to coat. Makes 6 cups (1.5 L).

Spiced Nuts

Cool completely. Store any extra mixture in a covered container.

1.	Butter or hard margarine	2 tbsp.	30 mL
2.	Soy sauce	1 tsp.	5 mL
	Lemon juice, fresh or bottled	1 tsp.	5 mL
	Ground ginger	1/4 tsp.	1 mL
	Garlic powder	1/8 tsp.	0.5 mL
	Onion powder	1/8 tsp.	0.5 mL
	Salt	1/4 tsp.	1 mL
3.	Walnut or pecan halves	3/4 cup	175 mL
	Whole blanched almonds	3/4 cup	175 mL

1. Place the butter in the pie plate. Microwave on high (100%) for 20 to 30 seconds or until melted.

2. Add the next 6 ingredients. Stir well.

3. Add the nuts. Stir. Microwave on high (100%) for 2 minutes. Stir. Keep microwaving and stirring every 2 minutes until the nuts are toasted. This will take about 10 minutes. Use the oven mitts to remove the pie plate to the hot pad. Lay the paper towel on the large plate. Put the spiced nuts onto the paper towel to cool. Makes $1\frac{2}{3}$ cups (400 mL).

Pictured below.

Get ready, get set!

- 10 inch (25 cm) glass pie plate or small microwave-safe casserole dish
- measuring spoons
- microwave oven
- dry measures
- mixing spoon
- oven mitts
- hot pad
- large plate
- paper towel

Tasty Taco Snack

A wonderful spicy barbecue flavor. Almost like nuts and bolts.

- large microwave-safe bowl
- dry measures
- long-handled mixing spoon
- liquid measures
- microwave oven
- measuring spoons
- small mixing spoon
- oven mitts
- hot pad

1.	**Corn bran cereal squares**	**4 cups**	**1 L**
	O-shaped toasted oat cereal	**2 cups**	**500 mL**
	Thin pretzel sticks, broken in half	**1 cup**	**250 mL**
	Peanuts	**1 cup**	**250 mL**
2.	**Butter or hard margarine**	**¹/₃ cup**	**75 mL**
	Envelope taco seasoning mix	**1 × 1¹/₄ oz.**	**1 × 35 g**
	Dry grated Cheddar cheese powder	**1 tbsp.**	**15 mL**

1. Combine the first 4 ingredients in the bowl. Stir.

2. Put the butter into a 1 cup (250 mL) glass measure. Microwave on high (100%) for 1 minute to melt. Add the taco seasoning and the cheese. Stir to mix. Slowly pour the mixture over the cereal mixture. Stir until the cereal mixture is well coated. Microwave, uncovered, on high (100%) for 5 to 6 minutes, stirring after 3 minutes. The cereal should be crisp. If not, microwave on high (100%) for 1 minute more. Use the oven mitts to remove the bowl to the hot pad. Let cool before you eat. Makes 8 cups (2 L).

Puppy Chow Snack

This one is for you, not your four-legged friend!

1.	**Chocolate chips**	**1 cup**	**250 mL**
	Butter or hard margarine	**¼ cup**	**60 mL**
	Smooth peanut butter	**½ cup**	**125 mL**
2.	**Rice squares cereal (such as Crispix)**	**7 cups**	**1.75 L**
3.	**Icing (confectioner's) sugar**	**1½ cups**	**375 mL**

- small saucepan
- dry measures
- mixing spoon
- large bowl
- rubber spatula
- large paper bag

1. Melt the chocolate chips, butter and peanut butter together in the saucepan over medium heat. Stir well.

2. Put the cereal into the large bowl. Pour the melted chocolate mixture over the cereal, using the spatula. Toss to coat well.

3. Put the icing sugar into the paper bag. Pour the cereal mixture into the bag. Close the bag and shake to coat with the sugar. Let cool. Store any extra snack in a covered container. Makes 8½ cups (2.1 L).

Candied Popcorn

Sticky to work with, but worth the sticky situation.

- very large bowl
- dry measures
- measuring spoons
- 2 long-handled mixing spoons
- large microwave-safe bowl
- microwave oven
- waxed paper

1.	Popped corn (pop about ⅓ cup, 75 mL kernels)	**10 cups**	**2.5 L**
	Corn flakes cereal	**2 cups**	**500 mL**
	Butter or hard margarine, melted	**2 tbsp.**	**30 mL**
2.	Raspberry drink mix	**¼ cup**	**60 mL**
3.	Butter or hard margarine	**2 tbsp.**	**30 mL**
	Large marshmallows (about 36)	**8 oz.**	**250 g**
	Vanilla flavoring	**1 tsp.**	**5 mL**

1. Combine the popped corn, cereal and the first amount of butter in the very large bowl. Mix well.

2. Sprinkle the drink mix over. Stir well.

3. Put the second amount of butter and the marshmallows in the microwave-safe bowl. Microwave on high (100%) for 1½ to 2 minutes. Stir to melt all the marshmallows. Add the vanilla. Grease the mixing spoons. Pour the hot marshmallows over the popped corn mixture. Toss quickly with the greased spoons until lightly coated. Lay the waxed paper on the counter or working surface. Turn the popcorn mixture out onto the waxed paper. Separate into serving-size pieces. Let cool on waxed paper for 30 minutes. Makes 13 cups (3.25 L).

Pictured on page 55.

Toasted Granola  hot

Add any chopped dried fruits in place of the apricots and raisins.

1.			
	Large flake rolled oats (not instant)	2 cups	500 mL
	Medium unsweetened coconut	½ cup	125 mL
	Shelled roasted sunflower seeds	¼ cup	60 mL
	Finely chopped dried apricots	½ cup	125 mL
	Golden raisins	½ cup	125 mL
	Bran flakes cereal, crushed	½ cup	125 mL
	Brown sugar, packed	⅓ cup	75 mL
2.	Cooking oil	¼ cup	60 mL
	Water	2 tbsp.	30 mL
	Vanilla flavoring (or almond flavoring)	1 tsp.	5 mL

1. Turn the oven on to 300°F (150°C). Combine the first 7 ingredients in the bowl. Stir to mix.

2. Combine the cooking oil, water and vanilla in a small measuring cup. Mix. Pour the oil mixture over the granola mixture. Stir well. Pour the granola mixture into the ungreased pan. Bake on the center rack in the oven for 25 minutes, stirring frequently. Use the oven mitts to remove the pan to the wire rack. Cool before eating. Makes 5 cups (1.25 L).

Pictured below.

Get ready, get set!

- large bowl
- dry measures
- mixing spoon
- liquid measures
- measuring spoons
- 9 × 13 inch (22 × 33 cm) oblong pan
- oven mitts
- wire rack

Left: Toasted Granola, page 55
Right: Candied Popcorn, page 54

Nut 'N' Honey Candy (chill)

Fun to make and wholesome, too.

- small bowl
- dry measures
- measuring spoons
- mixing spoon
- waxed paper
- sharp knife

1.	**Crunchy peanut butter**	**¹/₄ cup**	**60 mL**
	Liquid honey	**3 tbsp.**	**50 mL**
	Lemon juice, fresh or bottled	**2 tsp.**	**10 mL**
2.	**Skim milk powder**	**¹/₂-²/₃ cup**	**125-150 mL**
3.	**Finely chopped raisins or other dried fruit**	**2 tbsp.**	**30 mL**
	Graham cracker crumbs or fine sweetened coconut	**3 tbsp.**	**50 mL**

1. Combine the peanut butter, honey and lemon juice in the bowl. Mix until well-blended.

2. Add the milk powder, a little at a time, until it makes a nice dough that is not sticky. Add a bit more milk powder, if necessary. You should be able to gather it up with your hands and it should feel like play dough.

3. Place the dough on the counter or working surface. Knead the dried fruit into the dough. Roll into a long 6 inch (15 cm) rope. Sprinkle the graham cracker crumbs or coconut onto the waxed paper. Roll the candy rope in the crumbs until well coated. Wrap in the waxed paper. Chill in the refrigerator for 30 minutes. Cut into ¹/₂ inch (12 mm) slices. Makes 24 candies.

No-Bake Treats

All Around S'Mores

Fast. Easy. Looks fabulous! Tastes fabulous!

1.	Round graham crackers	4	4
	Hazelnut chocolate spread		
	Large marshmallows, white	2	2
	or colored		

- table knife
- microwave-safe plate
- microwave oven

1. Spread all 4 crackers with the chocolate spread. Place 2 of the crackers on the plate. Place the marshmallows on top. Microwave on high (100%) for 15 seconds. Remove the plate from the microwave. Place the other 2 crackers on top of each marshmallow. Push down slightly until the marshmallows spread to the outer edges of the crackers. Makes 2 s'mores.

Variation #1: Use digestive biscuits or sugar cookies in place of graham crackers.

Variation #2: Sprinkle chocolate chips or butterscotch chips on the bottom of 2 of the crackers. Microwave on high (100%) for 1 minute. Place the marshmallows on top. Microwave on high (100%) for 10 seconds. Top with the second crackers.

Pictured below.

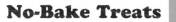

Corn Flakes Chews  chill

Keep these in the refrigerator unless you like 'em sticky.

1.			
	Liquid honey	¼ cup	60 mL
	Corn syrup	⅔ cup	150 mL
	Skim evaporated milk	¼ cup	60 mL

2.			
	Vanilla flavoring	1 tsp.	5 mL
	Corn flakes cereal	4 cups	1 L
	Angel flake (fancy flake) or long thread coconut	½ cup	125 mL

1. Combine the honey, syrup and milk in the saucepan. Stir over medium heat until the mixture starts to boil. Reduce the heat to medium-low. Simmer for 8 minutes. Do not stir. Remove the saucepan to the hot pad.

2. Add the vanilla, cereal and coconut. Stir to mix well. Cool for 10 minutes. Drop by rounded spoonfuls onto the waxed paper. Grease your fingers and shape and mound each chew into a nice stack. Chill for 30 minutes. Makes 24 chews.

Pictured on page 59.

- large saucepan
- liquid measures
- mixing spoon
- hot pad
- measuring spoons
- dry measures
- table spoon
- waxed paper

Scotch Rice Crunchies

A little fussy but fun to make—and even more fun to eat.

1.			
	Peanut butter, smooth or crunchy	½ cup	125 mL
	Butterscotch chips	2 cups	500 mL

2.			
	Rice squares cereal (such as Crispix)	3 cups	750 mL
	Miniature colored marshmallows	1 cup	250 mL

1. Put the peanut butter into the bowl. Microwave on high (100%) for 1 minute. Stir in the butterscotch chips. Microwave on high (100%) for 1 minute. Stir well. Microwave for 30 seconds more, if necessary, until the chips are melted.

2. Add the rice cereal. Stir until well coated. Stir in the marshmallows. Drop by spoonfuls onto the waxed paper. Makes 35 crunchies.

- large microwave-safe bowl
- dry measures
- microwave oven
- mixing spoon
- table spoon
- waxed paper

From top to bottom: Coated Marshmallows, page 63; Corn Flakes Chews, page 58; and Toasted Coconut Mallows, page 62.

No-Bake Treats

Puffed Wheat Candy Squares

Great any time of the day.

- large bowl
- dry measures
- 9 × 13 inch
  (22 × 33 cm)
  oblong pan
- medium saucepan
- measuring spoons
- liquid measures
- long-handled
  mixing spoon
- hot pad

1.	**Puffed wheat cereal**	**8 cups**	**2 L**
2.	**Butter or hard margarine**	**⅓ cup**	**75 mL**
	Golden corn syrup	**½ cup**	**125 mL**
	Liquid honey	**1 tsp.**	**5 mL**
	Smooth peanut butter	**1½ tbsp.**	**25 mL**
	Brown sugar, packed	**1 cup**	**250 mL**
3.	**Vanilla flavoring**	**1 tsp.**	**5 mL**
4.	**Butter or hard margarine**	**½ tsp.**	**2 mL**

1. Measure the puffed wheat into the bowl. Grease the pan.

2. Melt the first amount of butter in the saucepan over medium heat. Add the corn syrup, honey, peanut butter and brown sugar. Stir the mixture constantly over medium heat until it comes to a boil and the sugar is dissolved. This should take about 30 to 40 seconds. Remove the saucepan to the hot pad.

3. Stir in the vanilla. Carefully pour the sauce over the puffed wheat. Stir until the puffed wheat is well coated. Put the puffed wheat mixture into the pan.

4. Grease the palms of your hands with the second amount of butter. Press down and pack the puffed wheat firmly into the pan. Cool before cutting. Cuts into 24 pieces.

Pictured below.

No-Bake Treats

Peanut Butter & Banana Bars

These are good as a breakfast snack, too!

1.	**Chunky peanut butter**	**1 cup**	**250 mL**
	Liquid honey	**²/₃ cup**	**150 mL**
	Brown sugar, packed	**¹/₂ cup**	**125 mL**
2.	**Vanilla flavoring**	**¹/₂ tsp.**	**2 mL**
	Bran flakes cereal	**3 cups**	**750 mL**
	Dried banana chips	**1 cup**	**250 mL**
3.	**Butter or hard margarine**	**¹/₂ tsp.**	**2 mL**

- 9 × 13 inch (22 × 33 cm) oblong pan
- large saucepan
- dry measures
- liquid measures
- long-handled mixing spoon
- hot pad
- measuring spoons

1. Grease the bottom and sides of the pan. Put the peanut butter, honey and brown sugar into the saucepan. Stir the mixture over medium heat until it comes to a boil and the sugar is dissolved. Remove the saucepan to the hot pad.

2. Carefully stir in the vanilla. Add the bran flakes and the banana chips. Stir very well to coat the cereal. Put the mixture into the pan.

3. Grease the palms of your hand with the butter. Press down and pack the mixture firmly and evenly. Let it cool on the counter before cutting. Cuts into 24 snack bars.

Marshmallow Nests

These look like tiny nests with small marshmallow "eggs" inside. Very tasty.

- large microwave-safe bowl
- dry measures
- microwave oven
- mixing spoon
- table spoon
- waxed paper

1.	Smooth peanut butter	1 cup	250 mL
	Chocolate chips	1 cup	250 mL
2.	Large shredded wheat cereal biscuits	6	6
	Miniature marshmallows, white or colored	60	60

1. Put the peanut butter and the chocolate chips in the bowl. Microwave on high (100%) for 1 minute. Stir. Microwave on high (100%) for 1 minute more. Stir to melt the chips.

2. Crumble the wheat cereal biscuits into the chocolate mixture. Stir well until it is all coated. Drop by spoonfuls onto the waxed paper. Push 3 marshmallows into the middle of each. Form the nest around the marshmallows. Cool to harden. Makes 20 nests.

Pictured on the back cover.

Toasted Coconut Mallows  hot

Impress your friends with these!

- 9 × 9 inch (22 × 22 cm) square pan
- dry measures
- oven mitts
- mixing spoon
- hot pad
- small bowl
- large saucepan
- liquid measures
- long-handled barbecue fork
- paper towel
- waxed paper

1.	Medium unsweetened coconut	1 cup	250 mL
2.	Boiling water	4-6 cups	1-1.5 L
3.	Large marshmallows, white or colored	30	30

1. Turn the oven on to 350°F (175°C). Put the coconut into the ungreased pan. Bake on the center rack in the oven for 6 minutes or until golden, removing with the oven mitts to the hot pad every 2 minutes to stir. Cool. Transfer the toasted coconut to the bowl.

2. Put the water in the saucepan. Heat over high until mixture starts to boil. Reduce the heat to medium.

3. Use the barbecue fork to dip each marshmallow quickly into the boiling water. Dab the marshmallow on the paper towel then remove it from the fork and roll in the coconut. Set on the waxed paper to firm. Makes 30 marshmallow treats.

Pictured on page 59.

No-Bake Treats

Coated Marshmallows

Have your friends help you make these—and then enjoy!

1.	**Butter or hard margarine**	**1 tbsp.**	**15 mL**
	Golden corn syrup	**²/₃ cup**	**150 mL**
	Brown sugar, packed	**¹/₃ cup**	**75 mL**
2.	**Smooth peanut butter**	**¹/₂ cup**	**125 mL**
	Vanilla flavoring	**¹/₂ tsp.**	**2 mL**
3.	**Crisp rice cereal**	**5 cups**	**1.25 L**
4.	**Large marshmallows (white or colored)**	**24**	**24**

- small saucepan
- measuring spoons
- liquid measures
- dry measures
- mixing spoon
- hot pad
- large bowl
- table fork
- waxed paper

1. Melt the butter in the saucepan over medium heat. Add the corn syrup and the brown sugar. Stir until boiling. Remove the saucepan to the hot pad.

2. Add the peanut butter. Stir until melted. Add the vanilla. Stir.

3. Put the cereal into the bowl.

4. Use the fork to dip each marshmallow into the peanut butter mixture until completely coated. Roll the coated marshmallows in the cereal. Place the coated marshmallows on the waxed paper to cool. Makes 24 marshmallows.

Pictured on page 59.

No-Bake Treats

Peanut Oatmeal Nuggets  chill

Chewy and crunchy.

- large saucepan
- dry measures
- liquid measures
- long-handled mixing spoon
- hot pad
- measuring spoons
- baking sheet
- waxed paper
- table spoon

1.	Granulated sugar	1½ cups	375 mL
	Cocoa powder (not instant chocolate drink mix)	⅓ cup	75 mL
	Skim evaporated milk	½ cup	125 mL
	Butter or hard margarine	¼ cup	60 mL
2.	Peanut butter, smooth or crunchy	¼ cup	60 mL
3.	Vanilla flavoring	1 tsp.	5 mL
	Rolled oats (not instant)	2 cups	500 mL
	Chopped peanuts	½ cup	125 mL
	Medium unsweetened coconut	1½ cups	375 mL

1. Combine the sugar, cocoa, milk and butter in the saucepan. Heat and stir over medium until the mixture comes to a full rolling boil. Remove the saucepan to the hot pad.

2. Add the peanut butter. Stir until it melts.

3. Add the vanilla, rolled oats, peanuts and coconut. Mix well. Cut the waxed paper to fit the baking sheet. Lay the waxed paper on the ungreased baking sheet. Drop the batter by spoonfuls onto the waxed paper. Chill in the refrigerator until completely cooled. Store in a covered container in the refrigerator. Makes 4 dozen nuggets.

No-Bake Treats

Peanut Butter Candy (chill)

These are neat little peanut butter balls.

1.	**Peanut butter, smooth or crunchy**	²/₃ **cup**	**150 mL**
	Granola	³/₄ **cup**	**175 mL**
	Skim milk powder	¹/₃ **cup**	**75 mL**
	Brown sugar	**1 tbsp.**	**15 mL**
2.	**Mini chocolate or multi-colored baking chips**	¹/₂ **cup**	**125 mL**
3.	**Graham cracker crumbs, Oreo cookie crumbs, chocolate sprinkles or fine coconut, for coating**	¹/₂ **cup**	**125 mL**

Get ready, get set!

- medium bowl
- dry measures
- measuring spoons
- mixing spoon
- small bowl

1. Put the peanut butter in the medium bowl. Add the granola, milk powder and brown sugar. Mix well. Work in with your hands.

2. Add the chips. Mix in well. Form into 1 inch (2.5 cm) balls.

3. Place your choice of coating in the small bowl. Roll the balls in the coating. Cool and store in a covered container in the refrigerator. Makes 28 balls.

Variation: Use ¹/₂ cup (125 mL) of chopped glazed cherries, dried apricots or raisins instead of the chips.

Pictured below.

Lemon Pudding Squares chill

Very lemon! Very fresh!

1.	Cold water	½ cup	125 mL
	Envelope unflavored gelatin	1 × ¼ oz.	1 × 7 g
2.	Lemon-flavored gelatin (jelly powder), 4 serving size	3 × 3 oz.	3 × 85 g
	Boiling water	2 cups	500 mL
3.	Milk	1 cup	250 mL
	Box of instant lemon pudding powder (4 serving size)	1	1

1. Put the cold water into one of the small bowls. Sprinkle the unflavored gelatin over the water. Stir. Let stand for 10 minutes to soften.

2. Put the lemon-flavored gelatin into the other small bowl. Pour the boiling water over. Stir to dissolve. Add the softened unflavored gelatin mixture to the lemon-flavored gelatin mixture. Stir together. Let stand for 30 minutes.

3. Add the milk to the pudding powder in the medium bowl. Whisk about 2 minutes, or until well blended. Pour the cooled gelatin mixture into the pudding mixture. Whisk together until the colors are evenly blended. Lightly grease the pan. Pour the mixture into the pan. Cool in the refrigerator for 15 minutes or until set. Cuts into 42 squares or use cookie cutters.

Variation #1: Use raspberry-flavored gelatin with instant chocolate pudding powder.

Variation #2: Use orange-flavored gelatin with instant banana pudding powder.

Get ready, get set!

- 2 small bowls
- liquid measures
- mixing spoon
- measuring spoons
- medium bowl
- whisk
- 9 × 13 inch (22 × 33 cm) oblong pan

No-Bake Treats

Pizza Pop-Ups (hot)

Perfect for after basketball practice or for video movie night.

1.	**Tomato sauce**	**¹/₂ cup**	**125 mL**
	Chopped pepperoni	**1 cup**	**250 mL**
	Finely chopped onion	**1 tbsp.**	**15 mL**
	Grated Parmesan cheese	**1 tbsp.**	**15 mL**
	Grated mozzarella cheese	**¹/₂ cup**	**125 mL**
2.	**Refrigerator flaky rolls (10 per container, such as Pillsbury)**	**12 oz.**	**340 g**

1. Turn the oven on to 350°F (175°C). Grease the muffin pan. Combine the first 5 ingredients in the bowl. Mix.

2. Separate the flaky rolls into 20 pieces. Place 1 piece of dough into the bottom of each of the 10 muffin cups. Push down with your finger to form a shell (If dough sticks to your finger, coat your finger with flour). Divide the pepperoni mixture among the 10 shells. Flatten the remaining 10 flaky roll pieces slightly and place over the pepperoni mixture. Push the edges down slightly. Bake on the center rack in the oven for 15 to 20 minutes. Use the oven mitts to remove the pan to the wire rack to cool. Makes 10 pop-ups.

Pictured below.

Get ready, get set!

- muffin pan (for 10 muffins)
- medium bowl
- dry measures
- measuring spoons
- mixing spoon
- oven mitts
- wire rack

Salsa Pizza hot

Salsa instead of pizza sauce—zippy!

- baking sheet
- measuring spoons
- dry measures
- oven mitts
- wire rack

1.	Pita bread (8 inch, 20 cm)	1	1
2.	Chunky salsa (mild, medium or hot)	2 tbsp.	30 mL
	Grated Cheddar or mozzarella cheese	$\frac{1}{3}$ cup	75 mL
	Diced red or green pepper (optional)	$\frac{1}{4}$ cup	60 mL

1. Turn the oven on to 400°F (205°C). Place the pita bread on the ungreased baking sheet. Flatten with your hand.

2. Spread the salsa on the pita bread using the back of the measuring spoon. Sprinkle with the cheese. Add the peppers. Bake on the center rack in the oven for about 10 minutes or until the cheese is melted and the edge of the pita is crisp. Use the oven mitts to remove the baking sheet to the wire rack. Let stand 2 minutes before cutting. Cuts into 6 wedges.

Pictured on page 71 and on the front cover.

Tomato Mozza Rounds

A kid's type bruschetta (pronounced broo-SKET-ah).

1.	Medium tomato, chopped	1	1
	Olive oil	1 tbsp.	15 mL
	Garlic powder	⅛ tsp.	0.5 mL
	Salt	¼ tsp.	1 mL
	Grated Parmesan cheese	2 tsp.	10 mL
	Dried sweet basil	1 tsp.	5 mL
2.	French bread slices (cut 1 inch, 2.5 cm thick)	2	2
3.	Grated mozzarella cheese	¼ cup	60 mL
	Black olives, sliced (optional)		

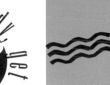

- small bowl
- measuring spoons
- mixing spoon
- baking sheet
- dry measures
- oven mitts
- wire rack

1. Place the rack in the oven in the top position. Turn the oven on to broil. Combine the first 6 ingredients in the bowl. Mix well.

2. Place the bread slices on the ungreased baking sheet. Broil on the top rack in the oven until browned. Use the oven mitts to remove the baking sheet to the wire rack to cool slightly. Turn the bread over and spoon the tomato mixture on the untoasted side of the bread.

3. Sprinkle with the cheese and olives. Broil for 2 minutes more or until the cheese is melted. Use the oven mitts to remove the baking sheet to the wire rack. Let stand for 1 minute. Makes 2 large rounds.

Pictured on the back cover.

Pita Pizza hot

If you like a thin-crust pizza this is the one for you.

- baking sheet
- measuring spoons
- dry measures
- oven mitts
- wire rack

1.	Pita bread (8 inch, 20 cm)	1	1
2.	Pizza or spaghetti sauce	2 tbsp.	30 mL
3.	Chopped cooked meat (ham, pepperoni, bacon or sausage)	2 tbsp.	30 mL
	Fresh mushrooms, chopped	2	2
	Grated mozzarella cheese	⅓ cup	75 mL
	Diced green pepper	2 tbsp.	30 mL

1. Place the rack in the oven in the top position. Turn the oven on to broil. Place the pita bread on the ungreased baking sheet. Flatten with your hand.

2. Spread the pizza sauce over the pita almost to the edges using the back of the measuring spoon.

3. Sprinkle the ham, mushrooms, cheese and green pepper over the sauce. Broil on the top rack in the oven for about 7 minutes or until the cheese is melted and the edge of the pita is crisp. Use the oven mitts to remove the baking sheet to the wire rack to cool. Cuts into 6 wedges.

Pictured on page 71.

Top: Pita Pizza, page 70. Bottom: Salsa Pizza, page 68.

Pizza Plus

Mini Pizzas 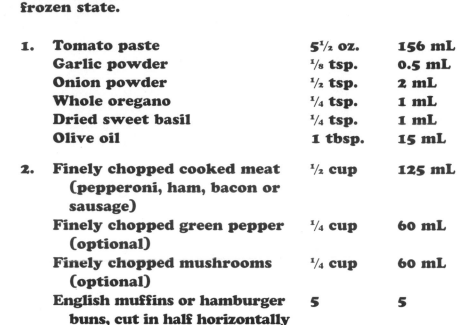 hot

Great when served immediately or cooked from the frozen state.

- small bowl
- measuring spoons
- mixing spoon
- dry measures
- baking sheet
- oven mitts
- wire rack

1.			
	Tomato paste	5½ oz.	156 mL
	Garlic powder	⅛ tsp.	0.5 mL
	Onion powder	½ tsp.	2 mL
	Whole oregano	¼ tsp.	1 mL
	Dried sweet basil	¼ tsp.	1 mL
	Olive oil	1 tbsp.	15 mL
2.	Finely chopped cooked meat (pepperoni, ham, bacon or sausage)	½ cup	125 mL
	Finely chopped green pepper (optional)	¼ cup	60 mL
	Finely chopped mushrooms (optional)	¼ cup	60 mL
	English muffins or hamburger buns, cut in half horizontally	5	5
3.	Grated mozzarella cheese	1 cup	250 mL

1. Turn the oven on to 350°F (175°C). Combine the first 6 ingredients in the bowl. Stir to mix well.

2. Add the meat, green pepper and mushrooms. Divide the mixture among the muffin or bun halves. Place on the ungreased baking sheet.

3. Sprinkle with the mozzarella cheese. Bake on the center rack in the oven for 10 minutes or until the cheese is melted. Use the oven mitts to remove the baking sheet to the wire rack to cool. (These can be wrapped airtight before baking and then frozen to be cooked as needed at 400°F, 205°C for 15 minutes). Makes 10 mini pizzas.

Pictured below.

Left: Mini Pizzas, page 72
Right: Pizza Burgers, page 73

Pizza Plus

Pizza Burgers  (hot)

Mom or Dad will like these, too!

1.	Wieners, chopped	2	2
	Finely chopped onion	¼ cup	60 mL
	Chopped mushrooms	½ cup	125 mL
	Finely chopped green pepper (optional)	¼ cup	60 mL
2.	Pizza sauce or tomato sauce	½ cup	125 mL
	Whole oregano	½ tsp.	2 mL
	Grated Parmesan cheese	2 tbsp.	30 mL
3.	Small cubes of Velveeta, mozzarella, or Cheddar cheese	⅓ cup	75 mL
	Kaiser buns or large hamburger buns, cut in half horizontally	3	3

- medium non-stick frying pan
- long-handled mixing spoon
- dry measures
- measuring spoons
- hot pad
- foil wrap
- oven mitts
- dinner plate

1. Turn the oven on to 350°F (175°C). Sauté the wieners in the frying pan for 1 minute over medium heat. Add the onion, mushrooms and green pepper. Stir. Cook for 5 minutes or until the onion is clear and soft.

2. Add the pizza sauce, oregano and Parmesan cheese. Stir. Remove the frying pan to the hot pad. Cool slightly.

3. Add the cheese. Divide the mixture generously on top of 3 of the bun halves. Top with the other bun halves. Press down slightly. Wrap each bun with the foil wrap. Bake on the center rack in the oven for 30 minutes. Use the oven mitts to remove the buns to the plate. Cool slightly. Makes 3 burgers.

Pictured on page 72.

Crispy Potato Wedges (hot)

These are great by themselves or with a dip.

- 9 x 9 inch (22 x 22 cm) square pan
- cutting board
- sharp knife
- pastry brush
- measuring spoons
- small cup
- mixing spoon
- oven mitts
- wire rack

1.	Medium potatoes, with or without peel	2	2
2.	Cooking oil	1 tbsp.	15 mL
3.	Onion powder	⅛ tsp.	0.5 mL
	Seasoning salt	¼ tsp.	1 mL
	Garlic powder	⅛ tsp.	0.5 mL
	Parsley flakes	¼ tsp.	1 mL

1. Turn the oven on to 450°F (230°C). Grease the pan. Slice the potatoes in half lengthwise on the cutting board. Cut each lengthwise half into 4 pieces to make a total of 8 wedges for each potato. Put the wedges into the pan and spread them around to make a single layer.

2. Brush the oil over the potatoes.

3. Combine the next 4 seasonings in the cup. Mix well. Sprinkle over the potatoes. Bake on the center rack in the oven for 30 minutes. Use the oven mitts to remove the pan to the wire rack. Stir the potatoes and spread out again. Bake for 10 minutes more or until crisp and golden. Use the oven mitts to remove the pan to the wire rack to cool. Serve with Creamy Yogurt Dip, page 29 or Hot Bean Dip, page 34. Makes 16 wedges.

Nacho Potato Chunks  hot

These have a great nacho kick to them.

1.	Medium potatoes, with peel	2	2
2.	Cooking oil	1 tbsp.	15 mL
	Taco seasoning mix (in envelope)	2 tbsp.	30 mL
	Sour cream, for dipping		

1. Turn the oven on to 450°F (230°C). Grease the pan. Slice the potatoes in half lengthwise on the cutting board. Slice each half crosswise into 4 pieces to make 8 chunks for each potato. Place in the bowl.

2. Drizzle the oil over the potatoes. Sprinkle with the taco seasoning. Stir to mix. Put into the pan and spread around to make a single layer. Bake on the center rack in the oven for 15 minutes. Use the oven mitts to remove the pan to the wire rack. Turn the oven temperature down to 400°F (205°C). Stir the potatoes and spread out again. Bake for 15 minutes more. Use the oven mitts to remove the pan to the wire rack to cool. Serve with sour cream. Serves 2 to 4.

Variation: Sprinkle with ½ cup (125 mL) grated Cheddar or Monterey Jack cheese before last baking time.

Pictured below.

Get ready, get set!

- 9 × 9 inch (22 × 22 cm) square pan
- cutting board
- sharp knife
- small bowl
- measuring spoons
- mixing spoon
- oven mitts
- wire rack

Pizza Plus

Pineapple Grilled Cheese

Quite a surprise inside!

- frying pan
- small cup
- measuring spoons
- mixing spoon
- table knife
- pancake lifter or metal spatula

1.	Canned crushed pineapple, well drained	2 tbsp.	30 mL
	Finely chopped pecans (optional)	2 tsp.	10 mL
2.	Process cheese slices	2	2
	White or whole wheat bread slices, buttered on one side	2	2

1. Heat the frying pan over medium-low. Combine the pineapple and pecans in the cup. Stir.

2. Put 1 cheese slice on the unbuttered side of 1 slice of bread. Spread the pineapple mixture on top of the cheese. Lay the second cheese slice over the pineapple. Lay the second bread slice, butter side up, on top of the cheese. Place the sandwich in the frying pan. When the bottom side is browned, flip the sandwich over to brown the other side. Use the lifter to remove the sandwich to the plate. Makes 1 sandwich.

Pictured below.

Top: French Jelly Sandwich, page 77
Bottom: Pineapple Grilled Cheese, page 76

Sandwiches & Salads

French Jelly Sandwich

Make for Mom and Dad on Saturday morning. Serve with syrup or sprinkle with icing sugar.

1.	White or whole wheat bread slices	2	2
	Jelly or jam (your favorite)	2 tbsp.	30 mL
2.	Large egg	1	1
	Milk	1 tbsp.	15 mL
	Granulated sugar	1 tsp.	5 mL
	Salt, sprinkle		
	Vanilla flavoring	¼ tsp.	1 mL
3.	Butter or hard margarine	1 tsp.	5 mL

- table knife
- measuring spoons
- 8 inch (20 cm) pie plate
- table fork
- non-stick frying pan
- pancake lifter

1. Spread the jelly on 1 bread slice. Cover with the other slice. Press down with your hand.

2. Beat the egg with the fork in the pie plate. Add the milk, sugar, salt and vanilla flavoring. Beat with the fork until blended. Dip both sides of the jelly sandwich into the egg mixture.

3. Melt the butter in the frying pan over medium heat until bubbling. Place the jelly sandwich in the butter. Cook until golden. Turn the sandwich over with the pancake lifter. Cook until golden. Makes 1 sandwich.

Pictured on page 76.

Toasty Tuna Torpedoes (hot)

These can be baked right away or make these ahead and freeze, then bake for 25 to 30 minutes.

1.	**Canned flaked tuna, drained**	7 oz.	198 g
	Grated Cheddar cheese	1 cup	250 mL
	Chopped dill pickle	2 tbsp.	30 mL
	Green onion, thinly sliced	1	1
2.	**Prepared mustard**	1 tbsp.	15 mL
	Mayonnaise (or salad dressing)	1 tbsp.	15 mL
3.	**Hot dog buns**	4	4

1. Turn the oven on to 350°F (175°C). Combine the tuna, cheese, pickle and onion in the bowl. Stir.

2. Add the mustard and mayonnaise. Stir.

3. Cut the hot dog buns horizontally on the cutting board, making sure you do not cut all the way through. Open the buns and stuff with the tuna mixture. Wrap in the foil. Bake on the center rack in the oven for 15 minutes. Use the oven mitts to remove the sandwiches to the plates. Cool each sandwich slightly before unwrapping. Makes 4 torpedoes.

Pictured on page 79.

- medium bowl
- dry measures
- measuring spoons
- mixing spoon
- cutting board
- bread knife
- 4 large pieces of foil
- oven mitts
- 4 small plates

Dill Pickle Sandwich

If you like dill pickles, you will love this sandwich!

1.	**Mayonnaise (or salad dressing)**	1 tbsp.	15 mL
	Bread slices	2	2
2.	**Medium-size dill pickles, cut lengthwise**	2-3	2-3

1. Spread ½ the mayonnaise on one side of each bread slice.

2. Lay dill pickle slices on 1 of the bread slices. Top with other slice of bread. Cut in half on the cutting board. Makes 1 sandwich.

Variation: Spread the bread slices with mustard instead of mayonnaise.

- measuring spoons
- table knife
- cutting board
- bread knife

Bean Quesadillas  hot

Hot in two ways! Quick and easy to make.

1.	White or whole wheat flour tortilla (10 inch, 25 cm size)	1	1
2.	Canned refried beans with chilies	⅓ cup	75 mL
3.	Small tomato	1	1
	Grated Cheddar cheese	½ cup	125 mL

1. Turn the oven on to 400°F (205°C). Lay the tortilla out flat on the ungreased baking sheet.

2. Spread the beans over the tortilla.

3. Cut the tomato in half on the cutting board. Gently squeeze over the paper towel to remove the seeds. Discard the seeds and juice. Dice the remaining tomato into small chunks. Sprinkle the diced tomato and cheese over ½ the beans. Fold the plain bean half over the bean, tomato and cheese half and press down lightly with your hand. Bake on the center rack in the oven for 10 minutes. Use the oven mitts to remove the baking sheet to the wire rack. Let stand for 3 to 5 minutes to set. Cuts into 6 yummy wedges.

Pictured below.

Top: Toasty Tuna Torpedoes, page 78. Bottom: Bean Quesadillas, page 79.

Get ready, get set!

- baking sheet
- dry measures
- table knife
- cutting board
- sharp knife
- paper towel
- oven mitts
- wire rack

Bean Burgers  hot

Make ahead and freeze the uncooked burgers after wrapping in the foil.

- medium bowl
- measuring spoons
- dry measures
- mixing spoon
- 4-5 large pieces of foil
- oven mitts
- 4 or 5 small plates

1.			
	Canned beans in tomato sauce	14 oz.	398 mL
	Ketchup	1 tbsp.	15 mL
	Prepared mustard	1 tsp.	5 mL
	Finely chopped onion	$\frac{1}{4}$ cup	60 mL
	Brown sugar	1 tsp.	5 mL
	Grated Cheddar cheese	$\frac{1}{2}$ cup	125 mL
2.	Hamburger buns, split	4-5	4-5

1. Turn the oven on to 350°F (175°C) oven. Combine the first 6 ingredients in the bowl. Mix.

2. Divide the mixture evenly among the bottom halves of the buns. Cover with the top halves. Wrap each bun tightly in the foil. Bake on the center rack in the oven for 20 minutes or until hot and the cheese is melted. Use the oven mitts to remove the burgers to the plates. Cool slightly before unwrapping. If cooking from the frozen state, bake for 35 minutes. Makes 4 or 5 burgers.

Sandwiches & Salads

Quick Banana Sandwich

A new "look" to the traditional peanut butter and banana sandwich.

1.	White or whole wheat bread slice	1	1
	Peanut butter, smooth or crunchy	1 tbsp.	15 mL
	Jam, your favorite	2 tsp.	10 mL
	Small ripe banana, peeled	1	1

- measuring spoons
- table knife
- wooden toothpick

1. Spread the peanut butter and jam on the slice of bread. Lay the banana diagonally across the middle of the bread. Bring the opposite corners of the bread slice up and fasten with the toothpick. Makes 1 sandwich.

Peanut Butter Log

Great for a fast after-school snack.

1.	Peanut butter, smooth or chunky	2 tbsp.	30 mL
	Cream cheese, softened (or spreadable fruit-flavored cream cheese)	1 tbsp.	15 mL
2.	White or whole wheat flour tortilla (10 inch, 25 cm size)	1	1
3.	Medium carrot, grated	1	1
	Golden raisins	2 tbsp.	30 mL

- small bowl
- measuring spoons
- mixing spoon
- table knife
- waxed paper

1. Cream the peanut butter and cream cheese together in the bowl using the spoon.

2. Spread the peanut butter mixture on one side of the tortilla.

3. Sprinkle the carrot and raisins over the peanut butter. Press down with your hand. Roll the tortilla up like a jelly roll. Wrap one end with waxed paper and eat with your hands. Makes 1 log.

Fruit Roll Tortillas chill

These will keep for several days in the fridge. A perfect snack for after school. Eat sliced or leave whole.

- small bowl
- table fork
- measuring spoons
- mixing spoon
- dry measures
- table knife
- plastic wrap

1.	Cream cheese, softened	4 oz.	125 g
2.	Icing (confectioner's) sugar	2 tbsp.	30 mL
	Canned crushed pineapple, well drained (see Tip)	8 oz.	227 mL
	Long thread coconut	¼ cup	60 mL
3.	White or whole wheat flour tortillas, (6 inch, 15 cm)	6	6

1. Put the cream cheese into the bowl. Mash the cheese with the fork until it is smooth.

2. Add the icing sugar, pineapple and coconut. Mix well.

3. Divide the mixture among the tortillas. Spread. Roll each tortilla up like a jelly roll. Cover with the plastic wrap. Place in the refrigerator for at least 1 hour. Cuts into 36, 1 inch (2.5 cm) pinwheels or 6 whole rolls.

Tip: Save the pineapple juice, chill and top up with some ginger ale and a cherry for a great beverage treat!

Pictured on the back cover.

Quesadillas  hot

The chunkier the salsa, the better!

1.	White or whole wheat flour tortilla (10 inch, 25 cm size)	1	1
2.	Chunky salsa (mild, medium or hot)	⅓ cup	75 mL
	Grated Cheddar cheese	⅓ cup	75 mL
3.	Sour cream (optional)		

1. Turn the oven on to 400°F (205°C). Lay the tortilla out flat on the ungreased baking sheet.

2. Spread ½ the tortilla with the salsa. Sprinkle with the cheese. Fold the other ½ of the tortilla over top of the cheese and press down lightly. Bake on the center rack in the oven for 4 minutes. Turn the quesadilla over using the pancake lifter. Bake for 4 minutes. Use the oven mitts to remove the baking sheet to the wire rack. Cool slightly.

3. Cuts into 3 wedges. Serve with a dollop of sour cream.

Pictured below.

Get ready, get set!

- baking sheet
- dry measures
- table knife
- pancake lifter or metal spatula
- oven mitts
- wire rack

Fruity Chicken Pitas

Store leftover filling in the refrigerator for 2 to 3 days.

Get ready, get set!

- medium bowl
- dry measures
- mixing spoon
- small bowl
- measuring spoons
- rubber spatula
- sharp knife

1.	Diced cooked chicken or turkey	1 cup	250 mL
	Small apple, cored and diced	1	1
	Canned pineapple tidbits, well drained	8 oz.	227 mL
	Crushed potato chips	1 cup	250 mL
2.	Mayonnaise (or salad dressing)	½ cup	125 mL
	Raisins	5 tbsp.	75 mL
	Ground cinnamon	¼ tsp.	1 mL
	Chopped walnuts (optional)	2 tbsp.	30 mL
3.	Mini pita breads	10	10

1. Combine the first 4 ingredients in the medium bowl. Stir.

2. Combine the next 4 ingredients in the small bowl. Mix. Fold the salad dressing mixture into the chicken mixture until coated.

3. Carefully slit each pita bread open at one end. Fill each pita "pocket" with ¼ cup (60 mL) of mixture. Makes 2½ cups (625 mL), enough for 10 pitas.

Pictured below.

Left: Salad Envelopes, page 85
Right: Fruity Chicken Pitas, page 84

Sandwiches & Salads

Salad Envelopes

A salad you can eat with your fingers.

1.	Medium tomato	1	1
2.	Grated carrot	¼ cup	60 mL
	Green onion, thinly sliced	1	1
	Thinly sliced green, yellow or red pepper (2 inch, 5 cm)	¼ cup	60 mL
	Grated Cheddar cheese	1 cup	250 mL
3.	Creamy dressing (your favorite)	2 tbsp.	30 mL
	Shredded iceberg lettuce	⅔ cup	150 mL
	White or whole wheat flour tortillas (10 inch, 25 cm size)	2	2

- cutting board
- sharp knife
- paper towel
- medium bowl
- dry measures
- mixing spoon
- measuring spoons
- 2 paper towels

1. Cut the tomato in half on the cutting board. Gently squeeze over the paper towel to remove the seeds. Discard the seeds and juice. Dice the tomato into 1 inch (2.5 cm) chunks.

2. Combine the tomato with the carrot, green onion, pepper and cheese in the bowl. Stir.

3. Add the dressing and toss the mixture together. Spread ½ of the lettuce down the middle of each tortilla. Leave some tortilla uncovered at one end to fold up envelope-style. Spread ½ of the veggie mixture over the lettuce. Fold the bottom of the tortilla up and then fold each side in. Leave the top open. Wrap in the paper towels to eat. Makes 2 envelopes.

Pictured on page 84.

Peaches 'N' Cream Salad

A mound of white on a bed of green.

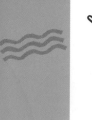

- small bowl or plate
- dry measures
- small spoon
- measuring spoons

1.	**Shredded crisp lettuce, handful**		
2.	**Creamed cottage cheese**	**½ cup**	**125 mL**
3.	**Canned peach slices, juice reserved**	**14 oz.**	**398 mL**
	Reserved peach juice	**1 tbsp.**	**15 mL**
	Maraschino cherry, for garnish		

1. Put the lettuce into the bowl or onto the plate.

2. Spoon the cottage cheese into the middle of the bed of lettuce.

3. Arrange the peach slices around the cottage cheese. Drizzle the peach juice over all. Top with the cherry. Serves 1.

Pictured on page 87.

FRUIT 'N' CREAM SALAD: Use canned fruit cocktail instead of peaches.

JAM 'N' CREAM SALAD: Use 1 tbsp. (15 mL) of jam on top if you don't have any fruit.

Sandwiches & Salads

Coconut Marshmallow Salad chill

A showy rainbow of color.

1.			
Miniature colored marshmallows	1 cup	250 mL
Canned fruit cocktail, well drained	14 oz.	398 mL
Canned mandarin oranges, well drained	10 oz.	284 mL
Long thread unsweetened coconut, white or colored	½ cup	125 mL
Maraschino cherries, halved (optional)	6	6
2. Sour cream or plain yogurt	1 cup	250 mL

- large bowl
- dry measures
- mixing spoon
- rubber spatula
- plastic wrap

1. Combine the marshmallows, drained fruits and coconut and cherries in the bowl. Stir.

2. Fold in the sour cream using the spatula. Cover the bowl with plastic wrap. Refrigerate for 30 minutes to allow the flavors to blend and the marshmallows to soften. Makes 4 cups (1 L).

Pictured below.

Left: Coconut Marshmallow Salad, page 87
Right: Peaches 'N' Cream Salad, page 86

Apple Grape Salad

Crunchy but not too sweet. You'll give this a thumbs up!

- medium bowl
- dry measures
- mixing spoon
- small bowl
- measuring spoons

1.	Red or green seedless grapes, halved	10	10
	Chopped walnuts (optional)	¼ cup	60 mL
	Thinly sliced celery	¼ cup	60 mL
	Small apple, cored and chopped	1	1
2.	Mayonnaise (or salad dressing)	2 tbsp.	30 mL
	Granulated sugar	1 tsp.	5 mL
	Lemon juice, fresh or bottled	1 tsp.	5 mL

1. Combine the first 4 ingredients in the medium bowl. Mix.

2. Combine the next 3 ingredients in the small bowl. Stir to mix well. Pour over the fruit mixture. Toss to coat lightly. Makes 1½ cups (375 mL).

Pictured below.

Sweet Cherry Buns

Great for a party snack.

1.	All-purpose flour	1½ cups	375 mL
	Baking powder	1 tbsp.	15 mL
	Salt	½ tsp.	2 mL
	Granulated sugar	2 tsp.	10 mL
2.	Milk	⅔ cup	150 mL
	Cooking oil	3 tbsp.	50 mL
3.	Granulated sugar	¼ cup	60 mL
	Ground cinnamon	½ tsp.	2 mL
4.	Cherry pie filling (or your favorite)	½ cup	125 mL
5.	GLAZE		
	Icing (confectioner's) sugar	½ cup	125 mL
	Almond flavoring drop	1	1
	Milk	4 tsp.	20 mL

- 10 inch (25 cm) pie plate
- medium bowl
- dry measures
- measuring spoons
- liquid measures
- mixing spoon
- table spoon
- small bowl
- small spoon
- oven mitts
- hot pad

1. Turn the oven on to 425°F (220°C). Grease the pie plate. Combine the first 4 ingredients in the medium bowl. Stir.

2. Add the milk and the cooking oil. Stir until moistened.

3. Mix the sugar and the cinnamon in the small bowl. Divide the batter into 12 mounds. Roll each mound, one at a time, in the sugar mixture. Coat each one, then place in the pie plate. Pat down lightly with your hand to make them touch each other. Make an indentation in the center of each one with your finger.

4. Spoon a heaping teaspoon of pie filling on top of each biscuit. Sprinkle with the remaining sugar mixture. Bake on the center rack in the oven for 14 minutes. Use the oven mitts to remove the pie plate to the wire rack.

5. **Glaze:** Combine all 3 ingredients in the 1 cup (250 mL) liquid measure. Mix until smooth. Hold the measure 12 inches (30 cm) above the hot buns. Pour a thin stream of glaze over all the buns using a back and forth motion. Let cool slightly. Makes 12.

Pictured on page 91.

Pictured on page 91.

Sweet Treats

Apple Pockets hot

Sweet and a bit gooey inside. Freeze any extras.

1.	**Crescent refrigerator rolls**	**2 x 8 oz.**	**2 x 235 g**
2.	**Small apple, cored and finely diced**	**1**	**1**
	Granulated sugar	**2 tbsp.**	**30 mL**
	Cinnamon	**½ tsp.**	**2 mL**
3.	**Icing (confectioner's) sugar**	**½ cup**	**125 mL**
	Vanilla flavoring	**½ tsp.**	**2 mL**
	Milk	**3 tsp.**	**15 mL**

1. Turn the oven on to 375°F (190°C). Grease the cake pan. Open the crescent rolls and separate into 16 triangles.

2. Combine the next 3 ingredients together in the bowl. Mix. Drop a small spoonful of the apple mixture near the wide end of each triangle. Fold the long points toward the middle over top of the filling. Pinch to seal. Fold over to the third point. Pinch to seal. Place 8 pockets, seam side down, in each cake pan. Bake on the center rack in the oven for 12 minutes or until golden. Use the oven mitts to remove the cake pan to the wire rack.

3. Combine the icing sugar, vanilla and milk in the plastic bag. Seal. Push down on bag to mix the ingredients together until smooth. Make a tiny cut across 1 corner of the bag with the scissors. Squeeze a zig zag pattern over each pastry. Makes 16 pockets.

Pictured on page 91.

Top: Apple Pockets, page 90
Bottom: Sweet Cherry Buns, page 89

Get ready, get set!

- 2 - 8 inch (20 cm) round cake pans
- small bowl
- measuring spoons
- dry measures
- small table spoon
- oven mitts
- wire rack
- small plastic sealable bag
- scissors

Sweet Treats

Hot Banana Boats

Eat with a spoon but be careful, it's a hot banana!

1.	**Firm ripe banana, unpeeled**	1	1
2.	**Chocolate chips (or other flavored baking chips)**	1 tbsp.	15 mL
	Miniature marshmallows (white or colored)	¼ cup	60 mL
3.	**Chopped walnuts or peanuts (optional)**	1 tsp.	5 mL

- cutting board
- sharp knife
- microwave-safe plate
- microwave oven

1. On the cutting board, cut the banana down the center lengthwise through the skin being careful not to cut through to the other side. Spread the banana open slightly. Lay on the plate, cut side up.

2. Sprinkle the chocolate chips and marshmallows inside the banana. Microwave on high (100%) for 1 minute 30 seconds. Remove the plate to the counter. Let stand 1 minute.

3. Sprinkle with the walnuts. Serves 1.

Sweet Treats

Microwave Baked Apple

Let an adult show you how to core the apple the first time you make this.

1. Medium or large red apple (McIntosh or Spartan is best)	1	1
2. Brown sugar	1 tbsp.	15 mL
Ground cinnamon	1/8 tsp.	0.5 mL
3. Butter or hard margarine	1 tsp.	5 mL

- vegetable peeler
- small microwave-safe bowl
- small cup
- measuring spoons
- small spoon

1. Wash the apple well and remove the stem. Pierce down into the middle of the apple several times with the vegetable peeler, digging out as much of the core as possible. Put the apple into the bowl.

2. Combine the sugar and the cinnamon in the cup. Stir. Sprinkle into the middle of the apple.

3. Top the apple with the butter. Microwave on high (100%) for 2 minutes or until the apple is tender. Cool slightly. Makes 1 apple.

Variation: For a chewy texture, use Crumble Topping, page 96, to fill the cavity of the apple instead of the brown sugar and cinnamon.

Pictured below.

Sweet Treats

Easy Rice Pudding

A favorite.

- medium microwave-safe bowl
- dry measures
- liquid measures
- measuring spoons
- mixing spoon
- microwave oven
- oven mitts
- hot pad

1.	Cooked white rice	1 cup	250 mL
	Skim evaporated milk (see Note)	½ cup	125 mL
	Milk	½ cup	125 mL
	Granulated sugar	1 tbsp.	15 mL
	Ground cinnamon, sprinkle		
	Raisins (optional)	¼ cup	60 mL
2.	Vanilla flavoring	1 tsp.	5 mL

1. Combine the first 6 ingredients in the bowl. Stir. Microwave, uncovered, on high (100%) for 3 minutes. Stir. Microwave on medium (50%) for 6 to 8 minutes or until the milk is absorbed. Use the oven mitts to remove the bowl to the hot pad.

2. Add the vanilla. Stir. The pudding will thicken as it cools. Makes 2 cups (500 mL).

Note: You can increase the milk to 1 cup (250 mL) if you don't want to use the evaporated milk.

Crunchy Maple Yogurt, page 96. Banana Pudding, page 95.

Sweet Treats

Banana Pudding

This has a lot of instructions, but it is really easy.

1.	**Milk**	**1½ cups**	**375 mL**
2.	**All-purpose flour**	**4 tsp.**	**20 mL**
	Cornstarch	**4 tsp.**	**20 mL**
	Granulated sugar	**½ cup**	**125 mL**
	Salt	**¼ tsp.**	**1 mL**
3.	**Milk**	**½ cup**	**125 mL**
4.	**Egg yolks (large), see Note**	**3**	**3**
	Butter or hard margarine	**1 tbsp.**	**15 mL**
	Vanilla flavoring	**1 tsp.**	**5 mL**
5.	**Banana, cut in ¼ inch (6 mm) slices**	**1**	**1**

- liquid measures
- microwave oven
- 1.5 quart (1.5 L) microwave-safe casserole dish
- measuring spoons
- dry measures
- mixing spoon
- whisk
- small bowl
- table fork
- plastic wrap

1. Put the first amount of milk into the 2 cups (500 ml) liquid measure. Microwave on high (100%) for 3 minutes or until hot.

2. Combine the flour, cornstarch, sugar and salt in the casserole dish. Mix well.

3. Add the second amount of milk and the flour mixture. Whisk slowly until blended. Add the hot milk. Whisk slowly until blended. Microwave on high (100%) for 4 minutes. Whisk. Microwave on medium (50%) power for 8 to 10 minutes or until pudding boils and thickens.

4. Beat the egg yolks together in the bowl with the fork. Slowly pour into the pudding while whisking. (If you do not add the egg yolks slowly, they will cook before they are blended and you will get scrambled eggs in your pudding!) Microwave on medium (50%) for 2 minutes.

5. Add the butter. Whisk until melted. Add the vanilla and sliced banana. Place the plastic wrap over the pudding. Cool. Makes 2⅔ cups (650 mL).

Note: As a suggestion, the egg whites can be used in Corn Flakes Macaroons, page 25.

Pictured on page 94.

Crunchy Maple Yogurt

Crumble Topping is great to sprinkle over yogurt, fruit or pudding. Just keep leftovers in a covered container in the refrigerator.

- medium microwave-safe bowl
- dry measures
- waxed paper
- microwave oven
- 2 mixing spoons
- oven mitts
- hot pad
- small mixing bowl
- measuring spoons
- 2 dessert bowls

1. CRUMBLE TOPPING		
Butter or hard margarine	¼ cup	60 mL
Rolled oats (not instant)	¾ cup	175 mL
Brown sugar, packed	¼ cup	60 mL
Graham cracker crumbs	¼ cup	60 mL
Long thread or fancy flake coconut	¼ cup	60 mL

2. MAPLE YOGURT		
Plain yogurt	8 oz.	250 g
Liquid honey	2 tsp.	10 mL
Maple extract (Mapleine)	¼ tsp.	1 mL

1. **Crumble Topping:** Put the butter into the microwave-safe bowl. Cover with the waxed paper. Microwave on high (100%) for 30 seconds. Add the next 4 ingredients. Mix well. Microwave on high (100%) for 30 seconds. Stir. Microwave on high (100%) for 30 seconds, or until nicely toasted. Use the oven mitts to remove the bowl to the hot pad. Break the mixture up as it cools.

2. **Maple Yogurt:** Mix all 3 ingredients in the small bowl. Divide between the 2 dessert bowls and sprinkle each with the Crumble Topping. Store any remaining topping in a covered container in the refrigerator. Serves 2.

Pictured on page 94.

Sweet Treats

Juice Jigglies

One is not enough!

1.	**Cold water**	**1½ cups**	**375 mL**
	Envelopes unflavored gelatin	**4 x ¼ oz.**	**4 x 7 g**
2.	**Frozen concentrated grape juice (or cranberry or raspberry cocktail), see Note**	**12 oz.**	**341 mL**

Get ready, get set!

- medium saucepan
- liquid measures
- long-handled mixing spoon
- hot pad
- 9 × 9 inch (22 × 22 cm) square pan

1. Put the water in the saucepan. Sprinkle the gelatin over top. Let stand 1 minute. Place the saucepan over medium heat. Bring the mixture to a boil, stirring frequently. Remove the saucepan to the hot pad.

2. Add the juice concentrate. Stir until dissolved. Grease the pan. Pour mixture into pan. Refrigerate for 1 to 2 hours until set. Cuts into 16 squares or use cookie cutters.

Note: Do not use a citrus concentrate such as orange, lemon or pineapple.

Pictured below.

Pineapple Sauce

Spoon over plain yogurt or use as an ice cream topping.

- medium saucepan
- long-handled mixing spoon
- dry measures
- measuring spoons
- small cup
- small spoon
- hot pad

1.	Canned crushed pineapple, with juice	14 oz.	398 mL
2.	Granulated sugar	$\frac{1}{4}$ cup	60 mL
	Cornstarch	2 tsp.	10 mL
3.	Maraschino cherries, cut into 4 pieces each	5	5
	Lemon juice, fresh or bottled	1 tsp.	5 mL

1. Heat and stir the pineapple in the saucepan over medium heat until it just starts to boil.

2. Combine the sugar and the cornstarch in the cup. Stir. Add to the pineapple. Stir until the mixture boils and thickens.

3. Add the cherries and lemon juice. Stir. Remove the saucepan to the hot pad. Let the sauce cool slightly. Cool completely in a covered container in the refrigerator. Serve chilled or at room temperature. Makes 1$\frac{3}{4}$ cups (425 mL).

Sweet Treats

Caramel Ice Cream Sauce

Rich and delicious. Serve warm or cold over ice cream.

1.	Brown sugar, packed	¾ cup	175 mL
	Golden corn syrup	⅓ cup	75 mL
	Salt, sprinkle		
2.	Skim evaporated milk	⅓ cup	75 mL

1. Combine the sugar, corn syrup and salt in the saucepan. Cook, stirring constantly, over medium heat until the mixture boils and the sugar is dissolved. Remove the saucepan to the hot pad. Let stand for 10 minutes.

2. Gradually stir in the milk until the sauce is smooth. Store any remaining sauce in a covered container in the refrigerator and reheat, if desired. Makes ¾ cup (175 mL).

- medium saucepan
- dry measures
- liquid measures
- long-handled mixing spoon
- hot pad

Hot Fudge Sauce

Delicious over ice cream or fruit. For all chocoholics.

1.	Bittersweet chocolate baking squares	4 x 1 oz.	4 x 28 g
2.	Granulated sugar	¼ cup	60 mL
	Salt, sprinkle		
	Skim evaporated milk	5 tbsp.	75 mL
	Vanilla flavoring	½ tsp.	2 mL
	Butter or hard margarine	1 tbsp.	15 mL

1. Break the baking squares in half and place in the bowl. Microwave on medium (50%) for 1 minute. Stir well to help melt the chocolate. Microwave on medium (50%) at 10 second intervals, stirring until the chocolate is melted.

2. Add the next 5 ingredients. Stir with the whisk. Microwave on medium (50%) for 30 seconds. Stir with the whisk. Microwave again on medium (50%) for 30 seconds. Stir with the whisk. Store any extra sauce in a covered container in the refrigerator. Reheat as needed. Makes ¾ cup (175 mL).

- microwave-safe bowl
- microwave oven
- mixing spoon
- dry measures
- measuring spoons
- whisk

Chocolate Chip Granola Bars  hot

Your mouth will water for these.

- 10 × 15 inch (25 × 38 cm) baking sheet
- large bowl
- dry measures
- liquid measures
- long-handled mixing spoon
- waxed paper
- oven mitts
- wire rack

1.			
Rolled oats (not instant)	3 cups	750 mL
Flaked almonds	1 cup	250 mL
Shelled sunflower seeds	1 cup	250 mL
Raisins	1 cup	250 mL
Chocolate chips	1 cup	250 mL
Sweetened condensed milk	11 oz.	300 mL
Butter or hard margarine, melted	¼ cup	60 mL

1. Turn the oven on to 325°F (160°C). Grease the baking sheet. Combine all 7 ingredients in the bowl. Mix very well. Mixture will be stiff. Put into the baking sheet. Press down evenly using the waxed paper. Bake on the center rack in the oven for 25 to 30 minutes or until golden. Use the oven mitts to remove baking sheet to wire rack. Cool for 15 minutes. Cuts into 20 bars.

Pictured below.

Sweet Treats

Chewy Peanut Bars  chill

These are just like a popular chocolate bar.

1.	Honey, liquid or creamed	¾ cup	175 mL
	Peanut butter, smooth or crunchy	1 cup	250 mL
2.	Chocolate chips	1 cup	250 mL
	Large marshmallows, white	10	10
3.	Crisp rice cereal	3 cups	750 mL
	Salted peanuts, finely chopped	1 cup	250 mL

1. Grease the pan. Combine the honey and the peanut butter in the saucepan. Cook over low heat until just boiling, stirring occasionally. Remove the saucepan to the hot pad.

2. Add the chips and the marshmallows. Stir until melted.

3. Add the rice cereal and the peanuts. Grease your hands slightly. Pack the peanut mixture into the pan, pressing firmly and evenly. Cool in the refrigerator. Cuts into 18 bars.

Pictured below.

Get ready, get set!

- 9 × 13 inch (22 × 33 cm) oblong pan
- large saucepan
- liquid measures
- dry measures
- long-handled mixing spoon
- hot pad

Wiener-Topped Baked Potatoes

Just right after a chilly walk home from school.

- table fork
- paper towel
- microwave oven
- measuring spoons
- non-stick frying pan
- mixing spoon
- hot pad
- liquid measures
- sharp knife
- cutting board
- two small plates

1.	Medium potato, scrubbed well	1	1
2.	Butter or hard margarine	1 tsp.	5 mL
	Wiener, sliced	1	1
	Chopped red pepper (optional)	1 tbsp.	15 mL
3.	All-purpose flour	2 tsp.	10 mL
	Milk	¼ cup	60 mL
4.	Process cheese spread (such as CheezWhiz) or grated Cheddar cheese	1 tbsp.	15 mL
	Hot pepper sauce, dash		
	Pepper, sprinkle		
	Sliced green onion, for garnish (optional)		

1. Poke the potato two times with the fork. Place the potato on the paper towel. Microwave on high (100%) for 2 minutes. Turn the potato over. Microwave on high (100%) for 2 minutes more or until the fork can be poked easily into the potato. Let stand while preparing the topping.

2. Melt the butter in the frying pan over medium heat. Add the wiener slices. Cook for 2 minutes, stirring occasionally. Add the red pepper. Stir for 1 minute. Remove the frying pan to the hot pad.

3. Sprinkle the flour over the mixture. Stir well. Add the milk. Heat over medium heat until bubbling and thickened.

4. Add the cheese, hot pepper sauce and pepper. Remove the frying pan to the hot pad. Cut the baked potato in half on the cutting board and place 1 half on each plate. Fluff each potato half with the fork. Spoon the cheese and wiener topping over each potato. Makes 2 baked potato snacks.

Rarebit Wieners (hot)

Lots of hot dog taste!

1.	**Hamburger buns, split and lightly toasted (see Note)**	2	2
2.	**Wieners, sliced**	2	2
	Grated Cheddar cheese	1/2 cup	125 mL
	Dry mustard powder	1/2 tsp.	2 mL
	Ketchup	1 tbsp.	15 mL
	Mayonnaise (or salad dressing)	1 tbsp.	15 mL
3.	**Paprika, sprinkle**		

- baking sheet
- small bowl,
- dry measures
- measuring spoons
- mixing spoon
- table knife
- oven mitts
- wire rack

1. Turn the oven on to 350°F (175°C). Place the bun halves, toasted side up, on the ungreased baking sheet.

2. Combine the next 5 ingredients in the bowl. Mix. Divide the mixture among the 4 bun halves. Spread and pack down with the table knife to cover to the edge of the buns.

3. Sprinkle lightly with the paprika. Bake on the center rack in the oven for 15 minutes or until the tops are bubbly and starting to brown. Use the oven mitts to remove the baking sheet to the wire rack. Makes 4 buns.

Note: Toast in a wide toaster, toaster oven or under the broiler.

Pictured on page 104.

Fried Onion Dogs

The onion really mellows and "sweetens" when cooked.

1.	Butter or hard margarine	2 tsp.	10 mL
	Small onion, peeled and cut into thin rings	1	1
	Wieners, cut into thin slices	2	2
2.	Hot dog buns, split open	2	2
	Mustard, ketchup and relish, to spread on bun (optional)		

1. Melt the butter in the frying pan over medium heat. Add the onion rings. Sauté for 3 minutes, stirring often, or until the onion starts to soften. Add the wiener slices and reduce the heat to low. Cook, stirring occasionally, for about 6 minutes or until the onion is soft and golden. Remove the frying pan to the hot pad.

2. Pile the mixture into the buns. Top with mustard, ketchup and relish, if desired. Makes 2 onion dogs.

Pictured below.

- frying pan
- long-handled mixing spoon
- measuring spoons
- hot pad

Left: Fried Onion Dogs, page 104. Right: Rarebit Wieners, page 103.

Wiener Snacks

Corn Dog Muffins hot

Good for lunch, too!

1.			
	All-purpose flour	1 cup	250 mL
	Cornmeal	⅔ cup	150 mL
	Granulated sugar	2 tbsp.	30 mL
	Baking powder	4 tsp.	20 mL
	Salt	½ tsp.	2 mL
2.	Wieners, diced in small pieces	6	6
	Large egg	1	1
	Cooking oil	¼ cup	60 mL
	Milk	1 cup	250 mL

1. Turn the oven on to 375°F (190°C). Grease the muffin pan. Combine the first 5 ingredients in the medium bowl. Stir together well.

2. Stir in the wieners. Beat the egg with the fork in the small bowl. Add the oil and the milk and beat all together with the fork. Add the egg mixture to the flour mixture. Stir to moisten. Do not stir too much. Divide the batter between the 12 muffin cups. Bake on the center rack in the oven for 20 minutes or until golden. The toothpick inserted in the center of 2 or 3 muffins should come out clean. Use the oven mitts to remove the muffin pan to the wire rack. Let stand for 10 minutes then remove the muffins to the rack to cool completely. Makes 12 muffins.

- muffin pan (for 12 muffins)
- medium bowl
- dry measures
- measuring spoons
- 2 mixing spoons
- small bowl
- table fork
- liquid measures
- wooden toothpick
- oven mitts
- wire rack

Wiener Boats  (hot)

Lots of options with this quick but filling snack.

- small cup
- measuring spoons
- mixing spoon
- table knife
- baking sheet
- 2 wooden toothpicks
- oven mitts
- wire rack

1.	Soft tub margarine	1 tbsp.	15 mL
	Garlic powder	⅛ tsp.	0.5 mL
	White or whole wheat bread slices	2	2
2.	Prepared mustard	2 tsp.	10 mL
	Process cheese slices (Cheddar, Swiss or mozzarella)	2	2
	Wieners	2	2

1. Turn the oven on to 350°F (175°C). Combine the margarine and the garlic powder in the cup. Mix. Spread on one side of each slice of bread. Lay the slices, buttered side down, on the ungreased baking sheet.

2. Spread the mustard on the unbuttered sides of the bread slices. Lay the wieners diagonally (from corner to corner) across each slice. Bring the two other corners together over the wieners. Pin together with the toothpicks. Bake on the center rack in the oven for 10 minutes or until the bread is toasty. Use the oven mitts to remove the baking sheet to the wire rack. Remove the toothpicks before eating. Makes 2 boats.

Variation #1: Spread each slice with 1 tsp. (5 mL) chili sauce or ketchup after spreading with, or instead of, the mustard.

Variation #2: Lay thin slices of dill pickle on either side of the wiener.

Wiener Snacks

Sneaky Snack

You can't get any easier than this. Have paper napkins handy.

1.	Wieners	2	2
2.	Jelly (grape, apple or red currant jelly)	1 tbsp.	15 mL
	Chili sauce or ketchup	1 tbsp.	15 mL

1. Cut each wiener into 6 or 7 pieces. Place all the pieces in the bowl.

2. Spoon the jelly and the chili sauce over the wiener slices. Stir to coat. Microwave on high (100%) for 2 minutes. Stir. Use the oven mitts to remove the bowl to the hot pad. Serve with the toothpicks to eat this snack. Serves 2 or 3.

Pictured below.

Get ready, get set!

- cutting board
- sharp knife
- shallow microwave-safe bowl
- measuring spoons
- mixing spoon
- microwave oven
- oven mitts
- hot pad
- wooden or cocktail toothpicks

measurement tables

Throughout this book measurements are given in Conventional and Metric measures. The tables below provide a quick reference for the standard measures, weights, temperatures, and sizes.

Spoons

Conventional Measure	Metric Standard Measure Millilitre (mL)
1/8 teaspoon (tsp.)	0.5 mL
1/4 teaspoon (tsp.)	1 mL
1/2 teaspoon (tsp.)	2 mL
1 teaspoon (tsp.)	5 mL
2 teaspoons (tsp.)	10 mL
1 tablespoon (tbsp.)	15 mL

Cups

Conventional Measure	Metric Standard Measure Millilitre (mL)
1/4 cup (4 tbsp.)	60 mL
1/3 cup (5 1/3 tbsp.)	75 mL
1/2 cup (8 tbsp.)	125 mL
2/3 cup (10 2/3 tbsp.)	150 mL
3/4 cup (12 tbsp.)	175 mL
1 cup (16 tbsp.)	250 mL
4 cups	1000 mL (1 L)

Weights

Ounces (oz.)	Grams (g)
1 oz.	30 g
2 oz.	55 g
3 oz.	85 g
4 oz.	125 g
5 oz.	140 g
6 oz.	170 g
7 oz.	200 g
8 oz.	250 g
16 oz. (1 lb.)	454 g
32 oz. (2 lbs.)	900 g
35 oz. (2.2 lbs.)	1000 g (1 kg)

Oven Temperatures

Fahrenheit (°F)	Celsius (°C)
175°	80°
200°	95°
225°	110°
250°	120°
275°	140°
300°	150°
325°	160°
350°	175°
375°	190°
400°	205°
425°	220°
450°	230°
475°	240°
500°	260°

Pans

Conventional Inches	Metric Centimetres
8x8 inch	20x20 cm
9x9 inch	22x22 cm
9x13 inch	22x33 cm
10x15 inch	25x38 cm
11x17 inch	28x43 cm
8x2 inch round	20x5 cm
9x2 inch round	22x5 cm
10x4 1/2 inch tube	25x11 cm
8x4x3 inch loaf	20x10x7 cm
9x5x3 inch loaf	22x12x7 cm

Casseroles

Conventional Quart (qt.)	Metric Litre (L)
1 qt.	1 L
1 1/2 qt.	1.5 L
2 qt.	2 L
2 1/2 qt.	2.5 L
3 qt.	3 L
4 qt.	4 L

index

creating

everyday recipes you can trust

From left to right: Orange Julius, page 11; Banana Berry Yogurt Shake, page 10; Peach Melba Float, page 12; Cranberry Frosty, page 10; and Creamy Fruit Slush, page 12.

Company's Coming cookbooks are available at retail locations everywhere. For information contact:

COMPANY'S COMING PUBLISHING LIMITED

Box 8037, Station "F"
Edmonton, Alberta
Canada T6H 4N9

Box 17870
San Diego, California
U.S.A. 92177-7870

TEL: (403) 450-6223
FAX: (403) 450-1857